# STYLEWISE

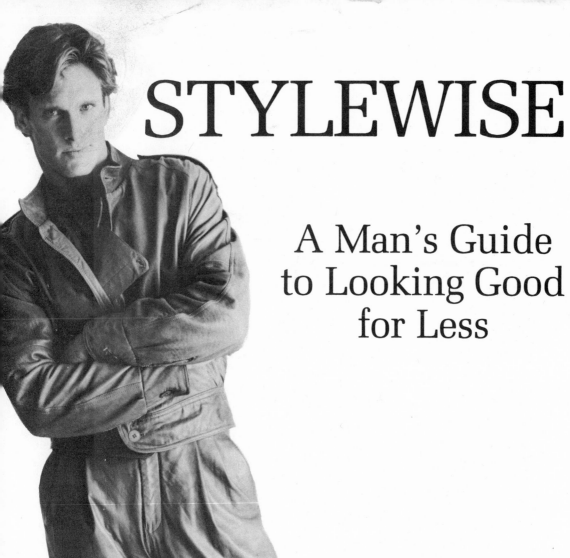

# STYLEWISE

## A Man's Guide to Looking Good for Less

## BY LEONARD McGILL

Photographs by Robert Whittington / Drawings by Robert Melendez

G. P. PUTNAM'S SONS
New York

Copyright © 1983 by Leonard McGill
All rights reserved. This book, or parts thereof, may not be reproduced
in any form without permission.
Published simultaneously in Canada by General Publishing Co. Limited, Toronto.

LIBRARY OF CONGRESS CATALOGING IN PUBLICATION DATA
McGill, Leonard, date.
    Stylewise.

    Includes index.
    1. Men's clothing.  2. Grooming for men.  I. Title.
TT617.M37 1983      646'.32      82-21513
ISBN 0-399-12792-5

DESIGNED BY HELEN BARROW
PRINTED IN THE UNITED STATES OF AMERICA

# ACKNOWLEDGMENTS

Half the fun of writing is meeting new and interesting people, and during the course of writing this book I've met dozens of exceptional individuals. Thank you all for your help and for making the project so enjoyable. I'm indebted to Editor-in-Chief Jack Haber and former Managing Editor Roger C. Sharpe of *Gentlemen's Quarterly* for giving me the chance to explore this book's subject for so long in that magazine's pages.

One group of people who deserve special thanks are the clothing manufacturers and retailers who lent clothes to be photographed. It takes guts and pride in your product to be featured in a book discussing trade "secrets" when you're in the trade. Thanks to the beautiful Royal Garden Hotel in Hong Kong and Pan American Airways for their excellent service, which was such a great help in researching the chapter on ordering clothes from "the fragrant harbor."

Thanks to my agent, Connie Clausen, and my editor, Diane Reverand, who believed in the project from the start and never let me or it down. Lastly, thanks to my wife, Doreen, for her support and patience. Without her help the idea for this project would have floundered like a bottle floating at sea.

*To my Mother and Father,*
*who taught me to reach*
*and be satisfied by the stretch.*

# CONTENTS

INTRODUCTION    11

## PART I / SHOPPING SMART

1 ▪ THE PRICE IS RIGHT    15
   Discount Shopping to Save

2 ▪ CLEAR SALE-ING    35
   Cleaning Up at Sales and Year-End Clearances

3 ▪ AN APPAREL SHANGRI-LA    46
   Custom-Made Clothes from Hong Kong

4 ▪ LONG-DISTANCE DIRECT    63
   Mail-Order Shopping to Save

5 ▪ SECONDHAND ROSES    85
   Used-Clothing Savings

6 ▪ MAN POWER    98
   How Clothing Salesmen Can Save You Money

7 ▪ WRONG BUT NOT FORGOTTEN    108
   Saving with Imperfect Apparel Bargains

## PART II / DRESSING SAVVY

8 ▪ CAPITAL GAINS    117
   The Investment Dressing Option

9 ▪ UNSEASONED VETERANS    129
    Building a Year-Round Wardrobe

10 ▪ ORIGINAL EQUIPMENT    138
    Active Wear as Street Wear

11 ▪ WORKING-CLASS HEROES    146
    Uniform Companies' Sturdy Savings

12 ▪ CORPORATE POSTURES    152
    Clothing as a Tax Deduction

PART III / MORE FOR THE MONEY

13 ▪ KEEPING IT TOGETHER    161
    Wardrobe Altering, Upkeep and Repair

14 ▪ IN THE TRIM    181
    Cutting the Cost of Great-Looking Hair

15 ▪ GROOMING TIPS    192
    Shaving Savings/Saving Scents/Home Based

CONCLUSION    203

STYLEWISE CLOTHES CREDITS    204

INDEX    205

# INTRODUCTION

THIS ISN'T a how-to-dress book. To find out how to tie a Windsor knot, whether or not to cuff your pants or what type of suit will make you look more powerful you'll have to look elsewhere. This is a book on saving up to 90 percent on the items you use in dressing and looking your best.

Today more men are interested in clothing and grooming as an enjoyable aspect of their lifestyles, just as they are interested in wine, food, travel, cars or tennis racquets. The problem is, now that men are interested in clothing, how can they afford it? A lot of people who supply you with your wardrobe components don't help much. As the men's fashion editor for a magazine with a huge national circulation once put it to me, "The whole men's clothing business is done with mirrors." Not quite. But there's a lot of room for the kind of hype that needlessly pads clothing prices. This book aims to break the mirrors, clear away the hype and point the way to prices stuffed with value.

While you'll find fifteen savings strategies outlined in the coming pages, dozens upon dozens of dress-for-less ideas are laid down. There's no one set plan or set of rules laid down. The ideas in one savings strategy may conflict with those in another. This isn't because one of them doesn't work; it's because no one set plan will achieve the best results for everyone. You'll have to pick and choose the strategies most appealing and relevant to you. In this way you'll save on dressing the way you want, whatever that way is.

The phrase "ignorance is bliss" might describe the way a lot of men now approach procuring wardrobe and image supplies. The modest goal of this book is to replace blind buying with informed insight. Keep your mind open to all the options, for little is gained from playing by conventional clothes-buying rules. After all, ignorance is bliss, but knowledge is freedom. And hopefully happiness, because when you start saving money when exercising your interest in looking good, the results are that much more enjoyable.

# Part I

# SHOPPING SMART

# THE PRICE IS RIGHT

## Discount Shopping
## to Save

MEN NEVER HAD IT so good. Discount-wise, that is. The legion of stores stocking quality menswear at a discount has doubled in number in recent years! If you're looking to dress better for less, shopping these value oases is a must move. In fact, I'd venture that for some clothing categories like basic sweaters, dress shirts, ties, underwear and socks, discounters are the only place to shop. It would have been lunacy to suggest such a course as little as five years ago. However, during those years discounting has radically restructured sartorial supply pipelines.

The original discounters sprang up in the fifties and sixties, paying about the same wholesale prices for their goods as regular-price retailers, but taking 10 to 20 percent less of a markup. They made their money by doing a volume business and by keeping overhead (store rent, store fixtures, sales help, etc.) to a minimum. They also tended to stock merchandise that was cheap, both quality- and price-wise, to begin with.

Today's menswear discounter is more likely to be what's technically termed an "off-price" retailer. He buys his merchandise below regular wholesale prices and passes these savings on to the customer. Regular-price retailers "keystone" prices, charging double the wholesale costs. For example, a big department store will buy a Calvin Klein suit at its regular wholesale price of, say, $149 and sell it to you for $289. An old-fashioned discounter probably wouldn't handle such a pricy item. If he did he would pay about the same $149, but, taking only an 80 percent markup, would charge you about $239. Today's off-price menswear store might only pay $100 for the same suit, and, taking an 80 percent markup, would sell it to you for $180. It's not unusual to find designer and name-brand suits and sport jackets selling at off-pricers for half what department stores charge.

# Monkey Business

The question, of course, is how off-pricers can get away with paying so much less for their goods. It's important to know, since most of us have learned that "if it's too good to be true, it *isn't* true." If something's less expensive it's inferior, right? Not at quality discounters.

Most people in the discount business are as shrewd as foxes on the run. They have to be. Theirs is a livelihood of backroom deals, quick, cool cash transactions, bluffs, risks and long shots that would make a pool hustler clammy. Who gets what from where varies wildly, but there's a mixed bag of identifiable methods.

Among them is buying manufacturer's overruns. These are the goods manufacturers are stuck with at the end of their selling seasons. Reasons for this vary: The item was overpriced to begin with, or wasn't pushed to store buyers in the right way, a steady customer didn't order as expected, a "hot" item from the previous season cools off. The result is 2,000 suits that must be sold *somewhere* fast, or 10,000 shirts that must be moved at cost to raise cash for production of next season's line.

Department and traditional menswear stores can't take advantage of the manufacturer's dilemma, because they usually order eight to twelve months before the season. For example, ordering fall sweaters in February. Off-pricers may wait until July or August (or later) to buy fall inventories, gaining access to overruns. Why don't department and specialty stores wait? Because they must plan their seasonal "fashion statements" and be assured of getting a full assortment of styles, colors and sizes.

Late buying used to be a strictly scavenger-type acquisition, but in some instances discounters are assuming a more symbiotic relationship with clothing makers. One reason for this is that department stores, like other large companies, take up to three months to pay for delivered goods. Cash-strapped clothing producers, even those who traditionally never sold to discounters, now do because many pay hard cash for overruns.

Another funnel opening each season through which your favorite name brand and designer fashions flow to discounters is the wide one carrying the canceled orders manufacturers must jettison. This can happen when a manufacturer is as little as a day late in shipping an order. A store can then refuse the goods. More cancellations appear when a store that ordered goes out of business. A discounter often pays 40 percent off regular wholesale prices to take what's deadweight to a manufacturer, but could be a fashion find for you.

A 65 percent discount is given off-pricers for handling manufacturer's "mistakes." Some of these are of dubious wearability, but not all are basket cases. For example, it's not unusual for a manufacturer to have a "bad run" of, say, 400 suits. The garments' sleeves may be short or their lapels not perfectly symmetrical. The flaw may be easily repaired or barely noticeable, but serious enough to warrant marking down the wholesale price.

Acting as safety valves for retailers as well, discounters buy clothes from other, higher priced merchants at the end of a selling season, when ritzy retailers' racks must be cleared. In these instances, discounters in effect sell last year's models.

Another way some discounters get the goods is by making their own bargains. A typical scenario: A name designer buys 7,000 yards of fabric to produce a certain sport shirt. However, he winds up using only 6,000 yards. A discounter steps in, buying the extra fabric at 40 percent less than its original wholesale price. He takes it to a small garment factory, where it's made up into up-to-the-minute-styled sport shirts that are sold as unlabeled, bargain-priced shirts. (Unfortunately, unwary bargain buffs can get burned when the purely profit minded use these same methods. An underhanded retailer will buy up the cheapest fabric imaginable. He will then take it to a factory that turns out clothes as finely crafted as the vegetable choppers advertised on late-night television. Undeniably bargain priced, such clothes are lucky if they survive their first rinse cycle.)

While overruns, cancellations, mistakes, leftovers and privately manufactured goods are all possible sources for savvy discounters, recently a more surefire method of getting off-price menswear has become popular. This is "early ordering," in which discounters order huge quantities of name-brand merchandise even before department stores, perhaps as far as a year before the clothes are made.

Manufacturers love such early orders because they generate a cash flow. Today many discounters are assured of all the off-priced goods they can sell, which is obviously great news for men savvy to such stores' bargain potential.

## Interior Decline

Someone once pointed out that discovering a juicy bargain at the typical menswear discounter was like seeing lobster thermidor on the local McDonald's menu. The incongruity between product and sales setting is often, to say the least, dramatic. The typical discounter's interior fixtures and displays have all the luxury of ball bearings. Clothes are hung on pipe racks or stuffed into table troughs under glaring lights as naked as they are bright. Signs are often hand lettered in red or black marker ink. Sales help is minimal, yet surprisingly helpful and knowledgeable. Dressing rooms are optional. In addition to the other refinements, a cash-only policy prevails.

The average Sears is sumptuously appointed compared to what are many times upgraded warehouses because low overhead helps keep prices rock bottom. You might think discount-store owners envy emporiums where merchandise nestles in a pleasant atmosphere and shows off on fancy mannequins. No way. Most

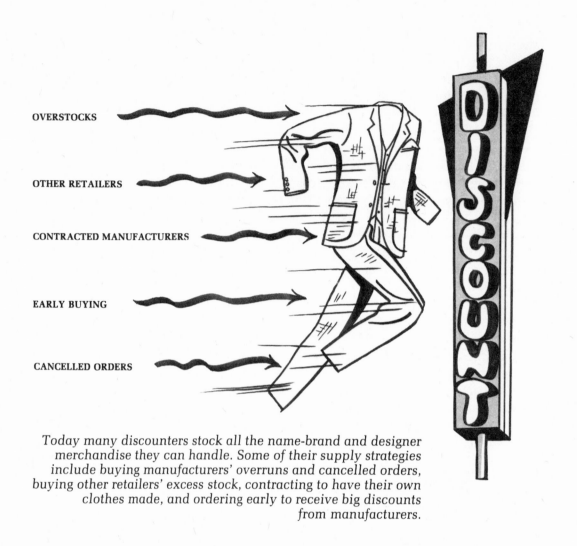

OVERSTOCKS

OTHER RETAILERS

CONTRACTED MANUFACTURERS

EARLY BUYING

CANCELLED ORDERS

*Today many discounters stock all the name-brand and designer merchandise they can handle. Some of their supply strategies include buying manufacturers' overruns and cancelled orders, buying other retailers' excess stock, contracting to have their own clothes made, and ordering early to receive big discounts from manufacturers.*

revel in the bare-bones approach. One, whose store's peeling brown paint and other nonamenities provide all the ambiance of a sweat shop, said he likes to see his designer merchandise in a factory-looking, warehouse setting because it creates "a mood of value."

Discounters also usually set up shop in a low- (or lower-) rent district, or on a 2nd, 3rd or 4th floor, where business costs are minuscule compared to malls or major shopping districts. Many discounters would like to be in better locations where increased store traffic would justify a higher rent, but most manufacturers will only sell to them if they're located outside major shopping areas and agree not to advertise. Otherwise, regular-priced retailers in the area would drop the manufacturer's line.

## As Time Goes By

Is it possible to frequent discounters comfortably and easily? More men answer "Yes" every day.

Fueling an increase in bargain hunting is the fact that the average Joe, whether or not he's willing to admit it, knows more about clothes today than five, ten or fifteen years ago. He's read more about them, knows more about what looks good on him and realizes dressing well is to some extent important or even enjoyable. These trends have helped create smarter shoppers, who recognize quality more easily. And it's a given: Whether you're buying a $36,000 Mercedes for $30,000 or a $20 polo shirt for $14, saving money feels oh so good.

## Play or Pay

Discount shopping can work for you. That is, unless you feel shopping ranks with dental visits and fixing flat tires on the recreation meter. Lots of guys feel this way. Given the chance, they'd choose bamboo slivers under the fingernails to hitting the suit racks and shirt bins. Maybe they (or you) were taught to hate shopping. Maybe it feels unmanly to concern yourself with it. Maybe it's just too big a hassle. Whatever, many men only manage to make it to a men's store once or twice a year, where they buy what they need before their 30-minute parking runs out. If this is you, forget discounters unless you're only buying three or four basic items per season. For example, two white dress shirts and two ties. And if you need something special, such as a wing-collar tuxedo shirt or a brown Harris tweed sport coat, and can only shop for it once, forget discounters. Their selections are usually too potluck for you to be able to get an entire season's worth of clothes or something specific in one or two outings.

A heavy dependence on discounters for wardrobe building works best for the frequent shopper (once a month or more) who can create a suitable personal image using gems of clothing collected from what are sometimes rocky fields. It's also fantastic for adding dramatic dimensions to basically solid clothing collections (that silk shirt you'd never buy at full price).

## Where the Buys Are

You never know what kind of clothes will turn up at local discounters. Their selection never ceases to surprise. Still, while the clothing constellation you can find at discount is wide and varied, not all of menswear's stars are readily viewed. In particular, high-priced European designer clothing, the kind chained to the racks in department stores, is rarely discounted, except when discounters buy out classy retailers' leftovers at the end of a season.

This doesn't mean you won't see names like Cerruti, Armani, Valentino or Versace. But these will be lines licensed by the designer, not his Italian or French made top-of-the-line merchandise. In licensing, designers usually sell their names to large clothing manufacturers. Sometimes they have a great deal of creative input into these lines. At other times they set general style directions and have final approval of fabrics and silhouettes. Still, European designers' licensed clothing is usually great stuff.

Apart from the Europeans' star models, the field is open, but some clothing categories predominate. As mentioned, sweaters, dress shirts, ties, underwear and

*Outerwear jackets and raincoats are plentiful at discounters.*

socks are usually in plentiful supply. And add outerwear to that list, too, especially raincoats. Of course, stores specializing in suits and sport jackets are stocked with bumper crops of them.

# Tipped Off

Now for some guerrilla tactics you can use to take discount stores by storm, as well as some common-sense tips:

• Taking some time to get to know salespeople pays off in almost any store you shop in. (See chapter 6.) You don't have to get on a first-name basis with a discounter's sales staff, but they harbor vital information, the kind that could put you in the thick of the store's best buys.

Here's why: Traditional stores receive new stock every few months. Discounters invariably receive smaller weekly shipments. If these are good, the best buys can be gone within 2–3 weeks. Knowing when they're coming gives you an edge. So ask salespeople, "Getting anything good in?" If they know, they won't mind telling you what and when.

• Don't bypass "irregulars" and "seconds" (see chapter 7). These must be clearly marked as such by law. An irregular is slightly flawed. A second is more seriously injured. But sometimes these are unbelievable buys, because the flaws may be minor and the merchandise perfectly wearable. Of course, examine such items extra carefully.

• After several visits to a discount store, you may start to feel its "rhythm." For example, you walk in and notice that the Yves Saint Laurent dress shirts filling three big tables two weeks ago are gone. They're replaced by dress shirts from another respected designer name. You notice there's another shipment of jogging suits, which are available every time you shop there. The price of a group of sweaters that have been there for a month or so is slashed in half. You realize most shipments that don't sell out right away are put on sale.

There is no one procedure or set of business practices to look for. But try to home in on store operations. Are a shipment's prices marked down after a month? Does the store always seem to stock certain clothing categories? Do they specialize in certain brands or designer labels? Getting a feeling for the store allows you to catch more sales and gives an idea of the clothing categories you can count on acquiring there.

• Lunch hours and weekends—times when you most want to shop—are the worst times to shop discounters. Cattle call, if you know what I mean. If you thrive in intense crowds, great. If not, try to hit stores at some other time, preferably in the morning, when clothes are still neat.

• Next to a $300 suit selling for $175 may be three $175 ringers selling for

$175. The best way to avoid them: check for quality (see chapter 8 for some tips of checking quality).

▪ Buying a lemon will sour your discount shopping days if it can't be returned. So know your rights. Some discounters will give back your money. Some will issue credit. Some will chuckle something about "let the buyer beware" while nixing either option. One discounter gives this advice: "People need to learn to read signs and labels. They should read a store's posted return policy. If it's not posted, they should ask." So beware. You shouldn't be surprised when you get home.

▪ Quite often, a man will inspect a garment—holding it up to the light, shaking it, rubbing its fabric—as if it held a secret for cutting his taxes in half. But get this same sleuth to try the thing on? Ha. It would be easier to get a Texan to twist instead of two-step. Mistake. When doing discounters *try everything* on. It's a good way to see if you really like it and quickly points up flaws in fit. If you can't try it on, make sure you can return it.

▪ You can cut down some of the scouting time spent at discounters by learning the lay of the bargain lands you've discovered. Merchandise is grouped in several ways: By type (suits, sport coats, pants, etc.), size, designer, price. After a while, quickly surveying the scene becomes second nature. At the beginning, look for a place where leftover stock is usually kept. This is a good place to start your shopping.

## Branded

There's one suspicion men have always harbored when shopping discounters: It's awfully hard to believe you're getting quality when everything around you indicates you're getting the bottom of the barrel. After all, would you buy a new car from a dealership with the trappings of a junkyard? Well, you just might if you saw it had half the sticker price of the same car sold out of a spotlessly clean car lot.

The moral: Once you know what you're getting the "selling environment" doesn't stop you from buying. Thus, buying a Calvin Klein suit at a discounter feels safer than buying something made by someone you've never heard of, just as buying a General Electric iron at an appliance discounter would. For this reason, most men become label watchers when they chart the discount sea. While there are some problems with this (which we'll discuss) most men lacking a well-developed eye for spotting good fabric, workmanship and style should adopt such a buying guideline, since sticking with labels recognized for providing such qualities puts them in good hands. One established discounter puts it this way: "An educated consumer is our best customer." But how can you tell the General Electrics from the unknowns? How do you become an educated menswear shopper?

Well, what would you do if you wanted to learn enough about wines to enable you to order a good wine with dinner? You might head to a reputable liquor/wine store and talk to salespeople about the differences between Bordeaux and Cabernet Sauvignons. You'd spend some time browsing among the store's racks, familiarizing yourself with vintages, bottlers, shippers, etc. And you might buy some books on the subject, and read articles about wines in magazines and newspapers when you came upon them. Somewhere down the road, when you wanted a dry, robust wine to go with your veal parmigiana, you'd be able to pluck one from a wine list with the wine steward's smiling approval.

The same dynamics apply to learning about one of life's basic necessities, your clothing. Your initial action can be poking through your closet, looking at labels on your favorite apparel. This starts you "thinking labels," and gives you some names to look for at discounters. The next step is field trips to your city's best department and men's specialty stores, which you *know* carry good to excellent sartorial stock. Unlike your usual visits your intention is to learn, not buy. So be more attentive, more curious. You're aiming to familiarize yourself with name brands and designer labels, their current styling and how much they cost. On one level this simply means equating name and price. (For example, Gant cotton dress shirt equals $24.) This way, if you see the same item discounted you'll know it's a bargain. On an advanced level you should be establishing relationships between a garment's construction, its fabric, its style and its price. This is learning to spot inherent quality, and it's difficult. You wouldn't expect a few trips to the wine store to make you a vino expert, so don't expect this to come overnight, either.

Reading helps. Several national magazines publish regular fashion features, including *Gentlemen's Quarterly, Esquire, Playboy* and *Penthouse.* And newspapers often run seasonal fashion sections in special Sunday supplements. Reading them and looking at the fashion photographs will help develop an eye for current styles.

After a while, names will begin to stick in the memory banks. But remember, all you really have to know are some reliable brands and the "normal" prices of their garments. Just for the record, here is a sampling of brands and designer labels with reputations for delivering quality: Alan Flusser, Alexander Julian, Bill Blass, Calvin Klein, Christian Dior, Daniel Hechter, Gant, Geoffrey Beene, Gianni Versace, Halston, Hart Schaffner & Marx, Hickey-Freeman, Lanvin, Lee, Levi Strauss, Jean-Paul Germain, Manhattan, McGregor, Munsingwear, Giorgio Armani, Pierre Cardin, Puritan, Nino Cerruti, Palm Beach, Petrocelli, Polo and Chaps by Ralph Lauren, Stanley Blacker, Tiger of Sweden, Valentino, Wrangler and Yves Saint Laurent.

# Missing in Action

Now the bad news. While labels are great tip-off tools, they're often removed by discounters as a concession to manufacturers. Why? In general, because garment makers would like you to buy from full-price operators, who buy from them at full wholesale prices. Also, they don't want a carefully calculated image tarnished. Somehow the pretentiousness, glamor, sexiness, etc., some manufacturers surround their products with fades when goods are displayed without frills at sane price levels. If a discounter doesn't remove labels on merchandise, and the same goods are carried at a nearby department store, there's likely to be trouble. The department store complains to the manufacturer, who in turn discontinues selling to the discounter.

What to do about label-less goods? The easiest thing to do is ask a salesperson who it's made by. They'll usually tell you. (This stretching of the rules doesn't seem to matter.) Then again, if you've seen the same garment at a full-price store or in a magazine, you'll know by whom it's made (that education comes in handy). Oftentimes, only part of the label has been taken out, and the remainder will be all the tag you'll need.

If all the above fails, you may yet discover who made a label-less garment. At least if it's a suit, which usually carries a large tag on the left sleeve. On the tag should be a WPL or RN number, which manufacturers are required to register with the Federal Trade Commission. Here's a sample listing of manufacturers' numbers you may find helpful in your discount shopping:

| | |
|---|---|
| Geoffrey Beene | RN 33293 |
| Stanley Blacker | RN 55639 |
| Bill Blass | RN 38344 |
| Pierre Cardin | RN 41858 |
| Oleg Cassini | WPL 9352 |
| Hart Schaffner & Marx | WPL 404 |
| | WPL 4001 |
| | WPL 4002 |
| Hickey-Freeman | RN 55075 |
| | RN 55077 |
| Calvin Klein | RN 54718 |
| Ralph Lauren (Polo) | RN 41381 |
| Palm Beach | WPL 4224 |
| | WPL 3133 |
| Petrocelli | WPL 6070 |
| | WPL 11849 |
| | WPL 11851 |
| | WPL 11853 |
| Yves Saint Laurent | RN 48545 |
| Van Gils | RN 49120 |
| | RN 57066 |

# Fake Out

What's in a name? To be sure, a designer label at a discounter whistles a hot prospect. *Sometimes*, however, the best thing about such finds is the label, which has been tacked on shoddy merchandise by clothing counterfeiters. Discounters are hotbeds for such fakery, because department and specialty stores usually enforce strict controls for spotting forgeries. Discounters may not. Fortunately, most counterfeiting in menswear is almost exclusively in designer jeans, because they are easily copied and produced.

How to spot fakes? Jeans priced ridiculously low are one tip-off. (When the counterfeiting phenomenon first surfaced, a Texas J. C. Penney made news when it unwittingly stocked phony Calvin Klein jeans priced at $5.99; their usual retail price is over $30.) But in many cases these could be just great deals. Your best bet is a quality control check of your own. Sloppy workmanship and an ill fit are two big tip-offs. One reason designer jeans are more expensive is the careful design, sizing and detailing that goes into them. Examine stitching. Is it even and neat? Zippers should be sturdy, not tinny. There shouldn't be a bunch of excess thread around buttonholes. There shouldn't be excess ragged fabric either. Try them on. Do they fit like the ones in the department stores? Check out the denim. Is it as thick and heavy as you'd expect? Another check: Do rivets have the designer's name stamped in? Lastly, are front pockets riveted? In other garments, fashion forgers usually simply affix counterfeit designer labels onto nondesigner merchandise. While this is rare, it's good to become familiar with authentic designer labels and emblems: their size, color, lettering and positioning on garments.

There's another name game you should be aware of. Starting in the early 1960s and exploding in the '70s, designer names have come to dominate menswear. Mostly, this has been healthy, as designer merchandise is usually more fashionable and better made. However, now every clothing manufacturer on the avenue wants to add a designer-licensed line. Trouble is, there just aren't enough "name" designers to go around. So manufacturers simply make up a French- or Italian-sounding name, like Jacques Laurent or Renaldo Picci. This merchandise isn't necessarily bad. (It had to be designed by someone, right?) But you're not getting the genius of, say, Pierre Cardin's group of designers or the quality most manufacturers back up a real big name with.

# Creative Outlets

Racing up the growth charts alongside discounters in recent years, "factory outlets" are beginning to change the way much of America shops. The idea is simple: manufacturers are becoming retailers. No middlemen. Big savings. The idea originated in New York's garment district more than sixty years ago. There, manufacturers began offering "seconds" to employees at cut-rate prices. Slowly, the idea spread to small industrial towns, often located in "the back country" of Pennsylvania and Massachusetts, where garments and other items were produced.

Then sometime in the early seventies things began changing. In 1972, a 200-store "outlet shopping mall" opened in Reading, Pennsylvania. It was so immediately popular that busloads of tourist/shoppers soon turned its shops into scenes thronged enough to make a riot squad squeamish. Similar malls are opening across the country every month, in older "rundown" shopping centers, on out-of-the-way stretches of interstate highways. In addition, outlet chains—some 100 strong—are stringing their way through the heartland. The new outlets aren't just havens for sad sack seconds, either. In fact, most are kept well stocked with first-quality merchandise by manufacturers who consistently overproduce to fill them. For manufacturers, the outlets provide ready cash and larger profits than selling to discounters.

The popular notion has it that outlets offer goods at wholesale. Rarely. Yes, on seconds and irregulars, you'll get 60 to 75 percent off regular retail. But on first-quality goods, the manufacturers running an outlet must take big enough markups to pay retailing cost (sales help, rent, fixtures, etc.). Therefore, expect only 25 to 45 percent off regular retail, which still isn't bad. Outlets usually excel in brand-name jeans, underwear, socks, sweaters and sportswear. They're not big on designer-name goods.

Following is a list of discounters, off-pricers and factory outlets selling menswear. The list is far from complete but may help you get started. For many more listings, several guide books are available. The only national guide to discount operations, listing over 2,000 stores carrying menswear, is Iris Ellis's S.O.S. (Save On Shopping) Directory. It will very likely pay for itself (as will other guides mentioned here) the first time you use it. (Write S.O.S. Directory, Inc., Box 10482, Jacksonville, FL 32207, for ordering information.) For men living in or visiting Ohio-Michigan; North and South Carolina; Washington, D.C.-Maryland-Virginia-Delaware; Pennsylvania; New Jersey; New York City or New England, Jean Bird's Factory Outlet Shopping Guides (they include all types of discounters) are comprehensive, indeed. (Write F.O.S.G. Publications, Box 239AM, Oradell, NJ 07649, for ordering information.) Now the list:

### ALABAMA

Van Heusen Outlet Store
1112 6th Avenue
Decatur

514 West Main
Dothan

614 South Commerce Street
Geneva

Munsingwear Factory Outlet
Highway 78
Guin

Bubba's Quality Discount Shoes
1743 Reese Street
Homewood

## ARIZONA

David Frank
7103 Stetson Drive
Scotsdale

The Hercules Employees Outlet Store
120 West Thomas
Phoenix

Second Serve
12416 North 28th Drive, Suite 8
Phoenix

## ARKANSAS

Carter's Factory Outlet
Pike Plaza
2706 Pike Avenue
Little Rock

Rhynecliffe Factory Outlet Store, Inc.
6100 Patterson
Little Rock

## CALIFORNIA

Beno's
1981 East Wright Circle
Anaheim

6815 Washington
Los Angeles

316 West E Street
San Diego

Clothing Clearance Center
2315 Fletcher Parkway
El Cajon

1057 South Olive Street
Los Angeles

2995 Junipero Serra Boulevard
Daly City

3918 Clairmont Square
San Diego

695 Bryant Avenue
San Francisco

942-A Blossom Hill Road
San Jose

255 El Portel Shopping Center
San Rablo

2660 El Camino Road
Santa Clara

Eric Ross and Company
9636 Brighton Way
Beverly Hills

Kauffman Enterprises
731 North Market Boulevard
Sacramento

Manufacturer's Clothing Outlet
360 Florida Street
San Francisco

Men's Fashion Depot
3740 Sports Arena Drive
San Diego

## COLORADO

Barry Manufacturing Company
200 South Santa Fe Drive
Denver

The Clothing Center
2222 South Havana Street
Aurora

245 East Jefferson Avenue
Englewood

## CONNECTICUT

Anders
20 Holmes Road
Newington

1535 John Fitch Boulevard
South Windsor

Frank Martin and Sons, Inc.
261 Main Street
Stamford

Leonard's Clothing Clearance
320 Boston Post Road
Orange

Main Modes, Inc.
1225 Connecticut Avenue
Bridgeport

Marshall's
Old Farm Shopping Exchange
West Main Street
Avon

National Brands Outlet
877 State Street
Westport

27

## DELAWARE

Murray's
4315 Governor Drintz Boulevard
Wilmington

101 Greenbank Road
Wilmington

## FLORIDA

Anders
2716 West Oakland Park Boulevard
Ft. Lauderdale

2004 Hollywood Boulevard
Hollywood

Benchmark IV
University Square Mall
Tampa

Blue Bell Factory Outlet
5880 Ramona Boulevard
Jacksonville

Cruise Casuals
2700 Southwest 8th Street
Miami

Direct Menswear
300 South Belcher Road
Clearwater

Fashion Clothiers, Inc.
2650 Northwest 5th Avenue
Miami

Jim Tatum's Men's Shop, Inc.
5318 Normandy Road
Jacksonville

Kuppenheimer Factory Store
515-1 East Altamonte Drive
Orlando

19 Sunshine Mall
Orlando

The Men's Room
2716 West Oakland Park Boulevard
Ft. Lauderdale

Peter Kent
560 Northwest 27th Street
Miami

Picasso Men's Clothing
576 Northwest 27th Street
Miami

## GEORGIA

Cumberland Men's Clothing Center
2653 Cobb Parkway Southwest
Atlanta

Frye Factory Outlet Store
800 Wharton Drive
Atlanta

Menswear Outlet
3343 Buford Highway Northeast
Atlanta

Menswear Outlet Northeast, Inc.
2514 Cobb Parkway
Smyrna

Menswear Outlet Three, Inc.
4610 Memorial Drive
Decatur

## ILLINOIS

Cheap Willy's Incorporated
One West Randolph Street
Chicago

1600 West Chicago Avenue
Chicago

4742 South Ashland
Chicago

Clothing Clearance Center
1224 Winston Plaza Shopping Center
Melrose Park

800 East Roosevelt Road
Lombard

273 Lawrence Wood Road
Niles

15645 South 71st Street
Orland Park

830 East Golf Road
Schaumberg

Independent Clothing Company
1313 South Michigan Avenue
Chicago

Irv's
2841 North Lawrence
Chicago

Men's Wearhouse
1400 South Clinton
Chicago

Rottapel Clothes, Inc.
531 West Roosevelt Road
Chicago

## INDIANA

The Company Store
West Lane Avenue
Indianapolis

Lawrence Bargain Center
8050 Pendelton Pike
Indianapolis

The Outlet, Inc.
5334 West 38th Street
Indianapolis

Walkers, Inc.
409 Market Plaza
Greenwood

## IOWA

Harry Lefstein, Inc.
327 Brady Street
Davenport

J. Brannam
3227 Southwest 14th Street
Des Moines

## KANSAS

Anders of Kansas City, Inc.
8850 West 95th Street
Overland Park

## KENTUCKY

Ashley's Outlet Store
500 New Circle Road Northwest
Lexington
2516 Plant Side Drive
Louisville

The Clothing Clearance Center
3041 Breckenridge Lane
Louisville

Cowden Factory Outlet
1318 Russel Cave Road
Lexington

## LOUISIANA

Clothing Showroom of Louisiana, Inc.
148 Carondelet Street
New Orleans

La Biche's Clothing
3840 Dublin Street
New Orleans

## MAINE

Marshall's
443 Western Avenue
Portland

## MARYLAND

Anders
832 Oregon Avenue
Liuthicum Heights
222 Northpoint Boulevard
Baltimore
2145 Greenspring Drive
Timonium

Batco Warehouse Shoe
6667 Moravia Park Drive
Baltimore

Hanover Shoe Factory Outlet
700A Merrit Boulevard
Baltimore

Sam Oidick and Sons
413 West Baltimore Street
Baltimore

Wall Street
5560 Randolph Road
Rockville
3112 Branch Avenue
Silver Hill

## MASSACHUSETTS

Adams
121 Beach Street
Boston
51 Union Street
Worcester

Charles S. Gellers & Son
68 Essex Street
Boston

Collinger, Inc.
350 Walnut Street
Agawan

Converse Rubber Company Factory
392 Pearl Street
Malden

Marshall's
160 Great Road
Bedford

Simon and Sons
South Shore Shopping Center
Braintree

## MICHIGAN

Clothing Clearance Center
Center Avenue
Bay City

Clothing Warehouse
511 West 11 Mile Road
Royal Oak

Great Lakes Sportswear Factory Outlet
Retail Store
11371 East State Fair
Detroit

United Shirt Factory Outlet
1927 Michigan Avenue
Detroit

## MINNESOTA

Ellis Men's Clothing
1335 Ellis Avenue
St. Paul

Kaplan Brothers
1435 Franklin Avenue E
Minneapolis

Nate's Clothing Company
25 North Fourth Street
Minneapolis

Milburn Clothing Company
1821 University Avenue
St. Paul

Milton Clothing
252 East 5th Street
St. Paul

## MISSOURI

Bob Jones Outlet
19th and Grand
Kansas City

Boyd's Subway West
7800 Forsyth
St. Louis

Famous Barr Going-Going-Gone Shop
6th and Olive
St. Louis

Gelber's Men's Store
7th Street and Columbia Plaza
St. Louis

J. Brannam
8700 East 63rd Street
Kansas City

Leonard Berin
222 South Bemiston
St. Louis

Marshall's
10780 Watson
St. Louis

## NEBRASKA

Ashley's Outlet Store
6121-25 Maple Street
Omaha

Kuppenheimer Factory Outlet Store
8411 West Center Road
Omaha

## NEW HAMPSHIRE

Adams Wholesale
189 South Broadway, Route 28
Salem

## NEW JERSEY

Adams of Pleasantville
Blackhorse Pike
Pleasantville

Bernies Ltd. of Passaic Park
103 Eisenhower Parkway
Livingston

The Casual Male
Route #130 at Riverton Road
Cinnaminson

Clothing Clearance Center
Route #18
East Brunswick

Jack Schwartz
516 Millburn Avenue
Short Hills

Leon Lustig
3 South Broad Street
Woodbury

Lloyds
21 East Palisade Avenue
Englewood

Munsingwear Factory Outlet
Glenwood Shop Highway
Burlington

## NEW MEXICO

Barry Manufacturing Company
2520 Jefferson Street Northeast
Albuquerque

Factory Outlet Store
2401 Ross Avenue Southeast
Albuquerque

## NEW YORK

BFO
149 5th Avenue
New York City

Brothers Clothing Shop
211-213 Main Street
White Plains

The Clothing Center
Brewerton Road, Route 11
North Syracuse

27 South Moger Avenue
Mt. Kisco

478 Ridge Road West
Rochester

2301 James Street
Syracuse

Clothing Factory Store
20 Voice Road
Carle Place

Dollar Bill's
99 East 42nd Street
New York City

H. Stanley Cord
195 East Post Road
White Plains

L. & S. Men's Clothing
580 5th Avenue, Room 510
New York City

Mo Ginsberg
162 5th Avenue
New York City

Parkway Men's Shop
52 Fulton Street
New York City

St. Laurie
84 5th Avenue
New York City

St. Michel Leatherwear
373 5th Avenue
New York City

Sussex Clothes Ltd.
895 Broadway
New York City

Syms
45 Park Place
New York City

## NORTH CAROLINA

Ashley's Outlet Store
Golden Gate Shopping Center
Greensboro

Barry Manufacturing Co.
4035 South Boulevard
Charlotte

Creighton Shirt Company Factory Outlet
4602 Market Street
Greensboro

Factory Suit Outlet, Inc.
2631 Battleground Avenue
Greensboro

Goofs Factory Outlet Pants Place
3722 East Independence Boulevard
Charlotte

Harvey Cannon, Ltd.
Long Leaf Mall
Wilmington

Milton's Clothing
163 East Franklin Street
Chapel Hill

6631 Morrison Boulevard
Charlotte

3934 West Market Street
Greensboro

## OHIO

Anders
43 East 6th Street
Cincinnati

5245 Ridge Avenue
Cincinnati

5107 Monroe Street
Toledo

Clothing Clearance Center
1028 South Smithville Road
Dayton

Straughn's For Men
171 Lincoln Way East
Massilon

## OKLAHOMA

Clothing Clearance Center
1675 South Yale
Tulsa

Famous Brands Clothing Outlet
181 Fairway Boulevard
Tulsa

190 South Hamilton Road
Tulsa

The Hercules Employees Outlet Store
2025 Corvair Boulevard
Tulsa

J. Brannam
4903-A East 41st Street
Tulsa

9797 East Admiral Place
Tulsa

Kuppenheimer Factory Outlet Store
6353 East 41st Street
Tulsa

The Shoe Factory
1080 Woodland Avenue
Tulsa

## OREGON

Anders
12160 Southwest Garden Place
Tigaro

825 Southwest 4th Street
Portland

## PENNSYLVANIA

Adam's Pier 36 Warehouse
Pier 36 North
Philadelphia

Route 202
Montgomeryville

Anders
Miracle Mile Shopping Center
Monroeville

942 Pennsylvania Avenue
Pittsburgh

641 Clairton Boulevard
Pittsburgh

1231 Roosevelt Avenue
York

Batco Warehouse Shoe Store
716 Adams Avenue
Philadelphia

Bendinger Brothers Men's Outlet Store
10 Shurs Lane
Philadelphia

D'ambrosio Clothing, Inc.
6405 North Broad Street
Philadelphia

House of Staley
723 Pennsylvania Avenue
Wilkinsburg

Middleshade Clothes
352 North 16th Street
Philadelphia

Rosoff's For Men
1714 Walnut Street
Philadelphia

## RHODE ISLAND

East Providence Clothing
360 Taunton Avenue
East Providence

H. S. Snyder Leather Factory Outlet
708 Elmwood Avenue
Providence

Pontiac Mills Factory Outlet
344 Knight Street
Providence

The Sweater Warehouse
212 Dartmouth Street
Providence

## SOUTH CAROLINA

Anders of Charleston
1714 Northbridge Terrace
Charleston

The Shoe Factory
1640 Highway #7
Charleston

## TENNESSEE

American Clothing Company
116 West Jackson Avenue
Knoxville

Ashley's Outlet Store
2721 Lebanon Road
Nashville

Barry Manufacturing Co.
323 Wilhagen Road
Nashville

Blue Bell Factory Outlet
338 River Rock Boulevard
Nashville

3536 Canada Road
Memphis

Gentlemen's Wear House Factory Outlet
3536 Canada Road
Memphis

Men's World Factory Outlet
4815 Kingston Pike West
Knoxville

Munsingwear Factory Outlet
3536 Canada Road
Memphis

309 River Rock Boulevard
Nashville

## TEXAS

Barry Manufacturing Company
13900 South Loop East
Houston

7280 Windwood
Houston

Country Boy Boots
1507 North Pruett
Houston

J. Brannam
2550 West Red Bird Lane
Dallas

404 North Town Mall
Dallas

and seven locations in Houston

J.D. Ranch Store
1408 West Davis
Dallas

2420 Gus Thomasson
Dallas

John's Boot Barn
16120 I-10 East
Houston

Merchant's Wholesale Exchange
1401 Fannin
Houston

Second Serve
438 State Highway 6 South
Houston

2709 Chimney Rocks
Houston

## UTAH

Barry Manufacturing Co.
2325 South 300 West Street
Salt Lake City

Brandell's
990 East 7200 South Street
Salt Lake City

The Factory Outlet
1800 South Redwood Road
Salt Lake City

VERMONT

The Clothes Hound
100 Main Street
Burlington

Dunham Factory Outlet
165 Church Street
Burlington

Hathaway Factory Outlet
153 Cherry Street
Burlington

VIRGINIA

Anders
6602 Virginia Beach Boulevard
Norfolk

617 McGuire Circle
Richmond

1800 West Broad Street
Richmond

Barry Manufacturing Company
Popular Hall Drive
Norfolk

Joseph A. Bank Clothiers
7259 Arlington Boulevard
Arlington

S. & K. Famous Brands
132 Virginia Beach Boulevard
Norfolk

5900 West Broad Street
Richmond

7110 Midlothian Turnpike
Richmond

4820 Azalea Mall
Richmond

Syms, Inc.
1000 East Broad Street
Arlington

Wall Street Clothing Factory Outlet
932 South Walter Reed Drive
Arlington

WASHINGTON

Anders of Lynwood
19800 44th Avenue West
Lynwood

WASHINGTON, D.C.

Joseph A. Banks Clothiers
1118 19th Street Northwest
Washington, D.C.

WEST VIRGINIA

Ashley's
Red Oak Shopping Center
Lewisburg

327 Main Street
Spender

114 First Street
Weston

Corbin Factory Outlet
5014 MacCorkle Avenue Southeast
Charleston

25th Street and Guyan Avenue
Huntington

WISCONSIN

Brill Brothers Inc.
2102 West Pierce Street
Milwaukee

Clothing Factory Outlet
1408 South Hastings Way
Eau Claire

Kahn's Clothing Outlet
602 North Broadway
Milwaukee

# ▪ 2 ▪

# CLEAR SALE-ING

## Cleaning Up at Sales
## and Year-End Clearances

FOR A LOT OF GUYS, sales are *it* as far as saving bucks on clothes. They just don't bother with any other savings strategy.

One reason for this approach: There are so many sales you could train for a marathon shopping them—Columbus Day, Labor Day, Presidents' Day, preinventory, postinventory, end-of-month, etc., etc.—not to mention events like "Moonlight Madness!" and "Cash-and-Carry!" where saving's scent swirls in a heady mix through the aisles and checkout lines.

Or, if you're of a more patient persuasion, the big end-of-season sales line up each year like ducks in a sale shooting gallery. Just sit back. Let the suckers buy clothes at full price. When the clearances come, you can mosey into the best shops in town and pay a sane man's price for your garb.

Yes indeed, for savvy shoppers sales are often happy trails leading to bins of bargains and deals on dapper apparel. But riding the sale trail right means more than trotting over to the nearest reduced-price clothes. Phrases like "drastically reduced" and "50 percent off" are meant to get us reaching for our wallets. But some questions should be answered before we do. For example, why do stores hold sales, anyway? We know stores have different names for sales. Are there different types of sales? (Yes.) Which are best? What's the best way to shop sales?

The bottom line on sales is certainly solid: With proper planning and smart shopping, anyone anywhere in the U.S. is likely to find the best men's clothing, at the best stores, for 15 to 75 percent off the original price. But making sales really work for you is another pie to slice.

# Cut Rates

Most men think merchants hold sales as a kind of last resort. After trying to get away with charging prices that would make an Arab sheik balk, the store is finally waving a white flag, begging for any business they can get by holding a sale. If you want to become a smarter sales shopper, file this notion under Erroneous Assumptions and read on.

Yes, it's true menswear shops and department stores don't like cutting prices. It's distasteful, and, worse, it cuts profits. But there's no way around it. It's as much a part of selling clothing as size markers and hangers. When a price is cut, the garment is said to be "marked down." A markdown is, when viewed unemotionally, simply a way for a clothes seller to correct the price of an item so it reflects a more realistic value.

There are as many reasons why prices are cut as there are menswear merchants. One often-sought objective is to maintain a well-groomed assortment of knitted and woven wares. This is a policy all quality department stores follow, and it inevitably leads to markdowns. The policy works like this: Stores reorder stock from manufacturers throughout the greater part of the selling season as they sell out of a style, color or size.

This is because customers, *especially* department store shoppers, demand variety. So in order to attain maximum sales, department stores are forced to carry more items than they can possibly dispose of before clearance season. Result: customer satisfaction, *and* lots of goods for you to pick from come sale time.

Another big reason for sales: They let a clothes purveyor keep his departments "clean," by ridding him of slow sellers or leftovers, in turn netting him cash to bring in new, fresh merchandise. After all, no store ever made a dime off a scarf or sweater sleeping on a shelf. Nothing happens until they're sold. So good stores like markdowns, because even though they're sold less profitably, they're cash creators. Along the same line, sales are used to bring people into the store. Nothing like a bargain to create "store traffic," and again, without customers, nothing gets sold. And of course, stores don't mind if customers drawn by a sale spend their savings on other, nonsale items.

Numbers are also lowered in the pricing game to adjust for earlier supply/ demand miscalculations. For example, a store buyer orders big into sweaters for a given fall season. The sweaters arrive, but the cold doesn't. As Indian summer runs into late October, the store starts sweating and marking down. Sometimes overbuying is purposefully implemented. For example, a store buyer is certain he can sell 500 white dress shirts at full price. He orders 600, knowing that even if he sells the extra 100 below full markup, he's sure to sell them on sale at a profit.

Men interested in exploring fashion's forward frontiers can sale away on another department store policy generating markdowns. Here's why: Big, prestigious

Stores like sales.
They generate store traffic
and start cash registers
ringing.

Items you'll find at end-of-season
clearance sales include basic wool sweaters,
scarves and corduroy pants at winter
clearances; summer sport shirts and shorts
at end-of-summer sales. European
designer goods, such as expensive,
stylish trench coats, are also often available.

department stores import European high-fashion looks to bolster their reputations as purveyors of high styles. But they don't expect to sell much of this rarified sartorial fare because its styling is too advanced, and because most people would rather buy a car or a boat with the kind of money such clothes cost. The result of carrying such great looking "window dressing": At season's end such goods—the Armani leather trench coats, the Valentino white wool overcoats, the Versace triple-pleated linen pants, the Missoni hand-knit ties—are often sold at a loss.

The last major markdown force is, in retail jargon, when certain garments become "nonoperational," meaning they become less than freshly minted—soiled with fingerprints, shorn of a button, returned in a wad, stained, or in the case of sets, broken up. Such injury-sidelined wear requires a markdown to sell.

As you can see, while the stores you most want to shop aren't particularly ecstatic over marking down prices, they nonetheless do it, and may do it often.

In fact, sales are getting easier to find. And the big seasonal menswear sales are starting earlier, lasting longer—even at the best stores. Several winds of change are creating these waves on the retail waters. Stores need to raise cash to cover the rising costs of printing and mailing sale circulars. In addition, sales are needed to counter (or try to counter) discount competition. Finally, the high cost of financing goods that often sit for months on storeroom floors and retail racks puts pressure on merchants to "turn" (or sell) goods as quickly as possible (in order to maximize investment dollars). The result of these three forces (plus the fact that men are becoming smarter consumers) is that less and less merchandise is being sold at full price. Today more than 40 percent of all men's clothing is bought on sale. For high-fashion items, it's more than 60 percent. And once you know how to shop them, sales can become a deep pool of savings, always ready to quench a thirst for bargains.

## Typecasting

Sales elicit a "thar she blows!" reaction in a lot of people. An excited feeling that a sale is a sale is a sale. Actually, every markdown is a bit different, designed by the store to achieve specific goals, along with the specific goal of making money. Every sale should be different for you, too. Playing your sale-shopping hand right means knowing the game you're being dealt. For example, if you know an end-of-month clearance is no more than a markdown of some of the store's regular stock you may not be as inclined to attend as you would a special-purchase sale, which is something quite different. Here, then, are the most common types of sales you'll encounter.

In special-purchase sales, department stores act like discounters (see chapter 1). Shirts, pants, suits or whatever are bought at below wholesale from a manufacturer and the savings are passed on to you. For example, a manufacturer is left with 700 camel's hair overcoats at the end of his selling season. A department store takes these off his hands for 30 percent below regular wholesale. It then advertises the coats as a special purchase and takes 25 percent off the regular retail price. *Note:* The store may already be carrying the camel's hair coat in stock when it gets the deal from the manufacturer. If so, the new goods will probably be mixed in with the old. Then, at season's end, the whole batch will be marked down to lower-than-normal sale prices.

In addition to special purchases, some department stores regularly schedule sales like the aforementioned end-of-the-month clearance, or preinventory, or assistant-managers' sales, etc. These are sales with which they try to catch your eye throughout the year. They offer bargains on clothes that are cold (as opposed to hot) tickets, or reductions on wearables that have been sprinting out the door, so that there are only "broken" sizes or less popular colors left (for example, a few larges but no smalls or mediums, or lots of black and orange but no navy or white). In such cases the store may not be able to reorder from the manufacturer; it decides to liquidate the remaining goods, generating cash and keeping the racks and bins looking sharp. Such miscellaneous price reductions are also used by some merchants to create goodwill with customers, in the same way stockbrokers treat their clients to lunch.

Menswear manufacturers can run sales themselves, and big, brand-name clothing producers sometimes sponsor yearly or twice yearly sales. This works the same way as when a food producer cuts his price by 25 cents, with the supermarket passing the savings along. Reductions are usually small (10 to 20 percent), but on a $200 or $300 suit the money could pay for a shirt and tie (if you got them on sale, of course).

Preclearance sales warm up the aisles before major end-of-season sellouts. They offer less dramatic bargains than real clearances, but more dramatic selections. The real things, the end-of-season clearances, are events seasoned sale shoppers anticipate with all the readiness of coiled rattlers. The biggest, the best sales, they warrant a thorough look.

## As Time Goes Buy

Patience is rewarded at end-of-season sales, as men who've learned to bide their time are treated to reduced prices at every shop in town. Buying off-season makes a lot of sense. Sales come with lots of time left in a season to wear your reduced-price prizes. And next year (if a garment can't be worn year round, see chapter 9), you'll have a nearly new garment waiting to greet the first cold snap or hot sun.

Now, you probably know the least expensive time to buy Christmas presents is in January, and the cheapest prices on bathing suits swim by in August. But to be a smart clearance shopper you've got to hone your timing. Spring/summer wearables check into stores in late January and throughout February. You'll find the first sales on these heat-treated goods in April, after Easter, when prices on slow movers are renegotiated. A greater variety of markdowns come in May (Memorial Day, especially), but die-hard clearance raiders hold off their charge until after the Fourth of July, when the big warm-weather reductions roll in. By the end of July, prices are lowest (but so are selections).

Fall/winter clothes follow a similar flow. They're brought into the store in late July and throughout August, and you'll find some sales in October and November, but because of Christmas buying, major clearances begin just before or after Christmas and throughout January.

The big end-of-season clearances, usually lasting four weeks, may be the only time you'll find the best stores' finest fare on sale. Because ritzy retailers and better men's specialty shops are blessed with clients willing to spend big on quality and style throughout the season, they follow "late-markdown" policies. This means holding only two large sales per year, in January and July, and taking only a few unadvertised markdowns in between.

The rationale: Bargain hunters, those crazed-eyed people normally avoiding ritzy retailers' ridiculous markups, are only attracted to the store twice a year. For the other ten months, the establishment's image is kept polished to a high gloss for regular-price buyers. In turn, because interim sales don't deplete stock, lots of clothes are available to make the two sales big events. But, again, even the best stores like these sales. After all, in January cold and snow keep shoppers (at least Northern shoppers) at home, and in July potential customers are sun worshiping, not shopping, so something must be done to start cash registers ringing.

Of the two major resources for menswear, department and men's specialty stores, department stores will usually offer the better clearance values. Smaller men's shops may have the storage space to pack away garments for six months. When the appropriate season rolls around again, the goods can go back out on the floor. Paradoxically, nearly all larger department stores liquidate their sartorial stock to free floor space and raise capital for the new season's inventory. Depending on the strength of their Christmas selling seasons, department stores begin winter/summer markdowns a week before or after Christmas/July 4th. Then, as January arrives, and July heats up, prices plunge further to as much as 75 percent off, to make way for the next season's styles.

# Finders Keepers

Here's what you can expect to find at end-of-season clearances:

*FORWARD FASHION.* As mentioned, prestigious department stores import European high-fashion looks to bolster their reputations as purveyors of high style. This merchandise is usually astronomically priced to begin with and therefore the first to be marked down. Initial cuts can be as high as 50 percent.

If you like exercising your sophisticated taste and fashion leadership, then snap up these markdowns faster than a cheetah on the run. There are few other savings strategies for obtaining such goods, as discount outlets don't usually handle them in quantity. In addition, they'll look even more "fashionable" next year, since some of their stylish details will have been copied by mass-market manufacturers.

*WARDROBE BASICS.* If your wardrobe is missing such winter essentials as corduroy pants, flannel shirts, wool scarves, Shetland crew neck sweaters, tweed sport coats and heavy outerwear, and summer staples like T-shirts, bathing suits, walking shorts, cotton pants, knit sport shirts and cotton sweaters, end-of-season sales are sweet sources to tap. By mid-January and mid-July, these basic wardrobe builders should be 50 percent off.

*SPECIAL-PURCHASE ASSORTMENTS.* End-of-season clearances often include special purchases (those, as mentioned, bought at below wholesale by the store and sold at a price reflecting this discount).

# Sales Savvy

As we've seen, the man looking to dress better for less can count on a variety of sales to help him. And, to aid him, a number of "guerrilla tactics" are available to get even more out of sale days. How best to breach the "Bargain Bonanza!" bins and raid the "Reduced!" racks varies with the event. If it's one of those "Moonlight Madness" happenings advertised in a way to create a frenzy among housewives, well, polish your armor. Under more rational conditions, here are some tips to help you shop sales more wisely.

- Take your own sneak preview of a sale. Shop the night before it starts, when salespeople are pricing garments for the next day. Sometimes, as soon as sale items are put out you can buy.
- If a presale shopping spree on the eve of an event is impossible, try to make it to the sale's first day. You'll usually find it offers the widest selection.
- Often, getting a jump on department store reductions is as easy as opening a

charge account at the store. This is because many department stores and men's clothing shops hold "private" sales for charge-account customers a week or so before advertising to the public. To take advantage of this practice, open charge accounts at your favorite stores following this procedure and get a first crack at sale items. But don't charge indiscriminately. And pay the bills before any interest is added. In short, you should treat the charge account as a delayed cash-payment system. Otherwise, finance charges will nix a portion of your savings.

• Some stores run weekly sales to bring in customers. These operations put good clothing on sale, hoping customers will spend more on "impulse" buying. Watch for such quality items in newspaper ads. When one of them is something you can use, buy it on sale.

• Stocking up on basics like T-shirts, socks, underwear, and white and light-blue dress shirts when they're on sale is a rational ritual. You'll always need these items. Why pay full price?

• As in other savings strategies, building up a friendly relationship with salesmen in your favorite stores is helpful come sale time, too. Your friends can clue you in on what's going on sale when. True, this strategy may be difficult to follow (who has time to shop, let alone become pals with salesmen?), but if implemented it will prove profitable.

• If you use a daily-planner-type note pad for scheduling business appointments, it's a great idea to jot down the dates of your favorite stores' sales as they occur. This will allow you to anticipate them next year (at the end of the year, transfer the dates to your new planner). While stores run sales on predictable schedules, they don't usually advertise them until the last minute.

• Related to the above: Time spent "scouting" a store's stock a week ahead of a scheduled sale (such as the week before July 4th) is time well invested. One reason is that you may hit an unadvertised preclearance sale. Another is you'll have time to browse, without jostling sale crowds, to locate the great goods you'll buy when they're reduced.

• Know that size-wise, mediums and small, in that order, are the first to disappear from sale shelves.

• It's easy at a fantastic sale to let your killer instincts take control. Rein them in. If you don't, you're likely to buy something because it's a great deal ("Look! A yellow velvet sport coat for only $40!"), realizing later you don't really care for it. ("I look like a walking lemon in it.") The general rule: Don't buy anything on sale you wouldn't buy at the regular price. The exception: Expensive items you couldn't afford at the regular price.

• Some high quality stores don't advertise their sales. Still, you'll be able to find items reduced in these stores at the end of each season. Leather goods specialists often don't advertise their sales, either. But savings of 30 to 50 percent are available there at season's end.

*Scouting a store's stock a week ahead of a scheduled sale*
*(such as the week before July 4th) is time well invested.*

▪ A warning, more than a tip, really: Don't expect good sales help. Salespeople, during large sales, are instructed to keep track of merchandise, take your money and keep things moving. Still, the store isn't giving anything away, so if you need help ask for it.

## Danger Signals

That last point is worth emphasizing: Sales offer bargains, but you're still laying out paper—often in big denominations—for whatever deals you discover. Some sales offer the best at the best prices. Still, when a store's main purpose is moving merchandise it's up to you to safeguard your wallet's holdings. So keep these thoughts in mind.

▪ Most stores have ironclad no return, no credit, no exchange, we-don't-want-to-see-your-face-here-again policies regarding sale items. To protect yourself, try everything on before buying—don't accept the size ticket's word. Also, check for imperfections. Often stuff on sale has been exposed to investigating hands for months, and the wear and tear sometimes shows. This is especially true of sweaters and knitted sport shirts, which usually have to suffer the indignity of being heaped on sales tables. On such sacrificial sale altars they're subjected to enough tugging to soften taffy. Fortunately, most pull through in great shape, but check 'em out inch by inch anyway.

• There may be an AS IS sign posted over a table of jumbled yet valiant-looking wearables. Something is no doubt wrong with each of them. It's up to you to determine if the defects are noticeable. But even if they are, consider having a tailor repair them (in the case of a missing button, for example). You may still save.

• Since special purchases are not part of the store's regular inventory there's a chance they may not be up to snuff quality-wise, so judge their inherent quality, not just price.

• You should be alert for retailers practicing a high initial markup policy. In this, a store sets prices on new clothes very high, knowing only a few will be sold at these inflated prices. After a few sales have been made the rest of the goods are "marked down" to normal markups. Then, at sale season, the prices of these same goods are "slashed" to normal sale prices. Avoid such a store until sale season, or altogether.

• The old "bait-and-switch" goes like this: A store advertises a garment, but when you get there you find they've sold out. (They probably only had a couple dozen to begin with.) A salesman then tries to sell you a higher priced "better" piece of clothing. Take a walk.

## Ad Ventures

Sale advertising is another area where knowing the game protects savvy shoppers from a stacked deck. Such advertising has a vocabulary all its own, seemingly penned by P. T. Barnum himself. For example, almost every time a sale price is given, it's compared to another, higher price. The big question: Is the former, higher price real, or did it materialize from an adman's daydream? To help answer that query, here's the Super! Colossal! *not to be missed!* wary-man's guide to sale-ad terms.

*List Price.* The retail price "suggested" by the manufacturer. This may be baloney. Yes, the garment maker may suggest a price. Usually, anyone trying to sell it for that price should wear a mask. A manufacturer can print any price on a shirt package, tie stick-on tag, etc., as a service to retailers, so they can produce the illusion you're getting a good deal. So the fact that a garment is "below list" doesn't guarantee a bargain. Ignore list prices. Look only at the sale price, comparing it to prices of similar items at other stores.

*Regularly Priced At* . . . Means the sale price is temporary, and the clothing will revert to a higher price once the sale is over.

*Originally* . . . Means once upon a time. Was it a year ago, six months ago, two weeks ago? Usually ads use "originally" when there have been several interim markdowns between the true original price and the current sale price.

*Comparable Value At* . . . Means the retailer *thinks* (or dreams) the garment is worth the quoted comparable price. Not that it ever sold or ever has a chance of selling at that price. This is a most nebulous phrase. Make your own comparisons.

*Everything Must Go!* Means the store owner wants very badly to sell everything in the store. But *not* because he's going out of business or *has* to sell out, only because he wants to make money.

*Going Out Of Business.* Again, this doesn't mean a store is necessarily closing down. (If this is the case, as you've probably observed, they usually mount posters in their windows counting down to the dreaded date.) Many stores "go out of business" for years, acting as liquidators, selling goods from stores or manufacturers that *have* bitten the dust.

*Special. Reduced. Clearance.* Mean there's a sale going on, but that can mean anything.

It must be said reputable stores don't engage in tricky advertising. And big department stores wouldn't last long if they employed it—people would just stop coming. Except in the case where a merchant is unknown to you, you can usually trust his advertising.

## Foot Joy

A last note on sales concerns shoes. They're perhaps the best items to buy on sale, as there are few other ways to save money on their purchase. Time is of the essence at shoe sales, as standard business and casual styles vanish fast, leaving only trendy and gimmicky models. Quality shoe shops regularly discount the wares by 15 to 50 percent at post-Christmas and early summer clearances.

One more note: Any man seeking to upgrade his sartorial front should shop sales. It doesn't make sense to buy fall clothes in August or summer gear in February. By biding your time, you'll get the same clothes for less, and only you'll be the wiser (and richer).

# AN APPAREL SHANGRI-LA

## Custom-Made Clothes
## from Hong Kong

HONG KONG. A name. A place. A richly colored, boat-filled harbor edging a beehive of shaded alleys, where fast-talking merchants offer exotic, dirt-cheap bargains. The port deserves its reputation as the East's discount mecca. And throughout the Crown Colony there's no bigger bargain than custom-made clothing—no other place on earth offers so much sartorial splendor for so little.

"So what?" you might ask. What good does it do you, since the cost of air fare to the Far East could buy your own tailoring shop? Just this: You can forget about astronomical air fares. You can prime a Hong Kong sartorial pump without ever going to the airport. How?

Some of Hong Kong's most respected tailors have set up mail-order operations servicing a worldwide clientele. The result: The ultimate savings strategy for acquiring custom-made clothes at a half to two-thirds off stateside prices.

## Strength in Numbers

A lot of men think custom-made clothes are something only the rich can afford. That's basically true, except for custom clothes from Hong Kong. For example, a custom-made suit for which you'd pay $1,200 on London's Savile Row, bastion of custom tailoring, or $600 in New York or Chicago, can be had from Hong Kong for about $300. How can Hong Kong be so much cheaper? Its "free port" status, low tax structure and the world's largest pool of tailoring talent make such

*Many Hong Kong tailoring establishments have been sewing their labels into fine custom clothing for over a quarter of a century.*

prices possible. The Crown Colony's phone directory lists five pages of tailoring establishments (New York's, on the other hand, one and a half), many employing well over two dozen masters of the cloth and thread. That's a lot of tailors.

These industrious suit shapers are carrying on a tradition of sartorial service established in the 1800s, when Chinese warlords ordered elaborate uniforms sewn by tailors on the small island off China's southern coast. Hong Kong tailoring became "Westernized" many years later, after England took possession of the island and a small inland area opposite it in the Opium Wars.

Wars, or rather warriors, have played pivotal parts in popularizing the port's custom trade ever since. For example, the British navy gave a big boost to the Hong Kong trade after WWI, as thousands of English seamen were custom outfitted. In those days custom work was the rule rather than the exception in Southeast Asia, where, traditionally, ready-made apparel was nearly nonexistent.

The quality of tailoring in Britain's "Pearl of the Orient" achieved worldwide acclaim in the late 1940s and early '50s, when many master tailors fled China's political revolution. Other wars, in Korea in the '50s and Vietnam in the '60s, gave many American soldiers a taste of the custom craft. And in the 1960s many of Hong Kong's top tailors began sending representatives worldwide, serving old clients and multitudes of new clients who'd seen their friends' unique bargain buys. Today, Hong Kong's custom clothing, the best for the money in the world, is available to everyone.

## On Your Own Terms

Hong Kong tailors let men who've acquired a taste for clothing cook up their own wardrobe feast. Ordering clothes incorporating your ideas and body measurements—made for you and nobody else—is the ultimate way to express your personal clothing viewpoints. If you like clothes, this is a supremely satisfying experience.

If you've never had clothes custom made for you, it's hard to imagine the quantum leap in satisfaction they can provide. First, there's fit. And custom means the perfect fit. How many times have you bought pants with too high a crotch, or a jacket that's too tight under the arms? Those things happen all the time with ready-made garments, almost never with custom. Custom entails shaping cloth to your body. This, of course, is a considerable advantage if you're not a standard size, for with custom-made clothes "irregular" shapes are no problem. Neither are extremely small or large sizes.

Apart from a personalized fit, ordering Hong Kong's custom clothing enables you to combine fabrics, styles and details as freely as a painter picks colors from a palette. You're given every possible option. (The exception: Exclusive fabrics from the world's top designers can't be had—but designer styling can usually be copied.) This solves the problem often encountered in ready-to-wear clothes, when you like the style, but not the color, or you like the color, but not the fit. In short, Hong Kong lets you be your own designer, letting you control not just how you wear clothes, but the clothes themselves.

Your garments become a direct reflection of your tastes. You don't have to adapt to some designer's viewpoint anymore. If you have the savvy, you can do it yourself. Men with higher incomes used to do this all the time. Hong Kong gives the guy who isn't wealthy the same chance. That's the bargain of this savings strategy. It's not so much the price, even though Hong Kong custom-mades are less expensive than suits of comparable quality in department stores, but the satisfaction of exercising your personal styling prerogatives.

And there are other lures to the Orient's intoxicating custom trade.

For example, old, worn wardrobe favorites can be copied exactly. (There's an old story about Hong Kong tailors' ability to copy garments precisely. A man brings his tailor a jacket to be copied. It being a hot day, he has a sweat-soaked handkerchief stuffed in the jacket's breast pocket. The new jacket is delivered—you guessed it—with a sweaty handkerchief in its breast pocket.)

For clothing afficionados, the amount of hand sewing involved in custom-made apparel is a real treat. This pays off in softer construction (clothes feel pliable, relaxed) and makes for such pleasurable details as hand-sewn buttonholes, working sleeve button closures and suits with perfectly matched plaids and stripes.

# Being There

There are three ways to set up a Hong Kong apparel connection. The simplest, of course, is to order your clothes when visiting the Crown Colony. I know, I know . . . I said you could forget about astronomical air fares. But it's a fact that "the fragrant harbor" is drawing more businessmen and tourists to its environs every year. Businessmen, because the port is the financial capital of Southeast Asia; tourists, to take advantage of the terrific shopping and to make entries into China.

Staying in Hong Kong is advantageous when ordering suits because producing a custom suit entails shaping fabric to your proportions. As a rule two fittings are scheduled to facilitate the shaping process. (With other garments this isn't as important. Shirts, for example, don't require any fittings.) One fitting takes place with the garment loosely stitched together. This enables the tailor to pin it into a more exact shape. The second fitting takes place with the suit sewn up, near completion, but with enough leeway to allow for more precise pinning. A third fitting takes place when the suit is done. If something is wrong, it can be corrected before delivery.

If you travel on pleasure to Hong Kong you may very well go by ship, and may stop at Singapore first. Frequently, cruise-ship personnel will arrange for a fitter to be available there to take your measurements. By the time the ship docks in Hong Kong a first fitting can take place. Also, travelers staying in large hotels throughout Southeast Asia will find they frequently have a house tailor. It's sometimes possible, if hotels are part of a chain with a branch in Hong Kong, to have measurements taken in, say, Bangkok, so that the first fitting will be possible when checking into your Hong Kong hotel.

Obviously, if you're not in Hong Kong you can't have fittings. Thus, a trip to the area remains the *best* way to take advantage of its tailoring trade.

## Traveling Tape

But other very viable options can bring the best in custom threads to your closet. For the uninitiated, visiting a traveling Hong Kong tailor gives hands-on experience with many basic ordering operations, and ensures a well-fitting finished garment. And nothing could be easier. Each year, many top tailoring firms send tailors to the United States and Europe to take orders. They make stops in fifteen to twenty major cities in the U.S., setting up shop in hotel rooms. To find out when such traveling tailors will be in your city, write to the firms listed in this chapter who send representatives stateside, requesting to be put on their mailing lists. They'll notify you when their man is coming.

When you visit him, you'll be able to choose from a selection of hundreds of sample suit, shirt, pant and coat fabrics. He'll also show you a style book. This includes many different garment styles, along with pages of specific styling details (such as a variety of shirt collars). You'll choose the fabrics, styles and details you want, the tailor will take your measurements and, perhaps, a photograph of you in your undershorts. In four to six weeks your clothes will be flown in from the Far East.

## Orders to Go

The third and most popular method for taking advantage of the Crown Colony's made-for-you menswear is ordering by mail. Over three million clients worldwide do just that. This includes men who've visited a Hong Kong tailor in the Orient or U.S. Once one suit is made for you, your measurements are kept on file, so any further orders only require choosing styles and fabrics. Joining the mail-order ranks is easy and, if caution is exercised, relatively safe (and if you live in an out-of-the-way location, a necessity).

Starting the Oriental apparel express moving requires writing to a firm, requesting an order form and sample fabric swatches. (This applies to the previously served as well as first timers.) Don't be concerned that you're writing in English. The companies listed in this book are bilingual and order forms are in English as well.

It costs a tailor about $5 to send you sample swatches. Most provide this service free, but it's a good idea for first-time customers to send a fiver. There are two advantages to this. One, you'll probably receive more samples sooner. Two, you'll establish your seriousness. What Hong Kong tailors dislike is receiving a photocopied letter requesting sample swatches. They see this as a "shopping around" tactic. They'll still send swatches, but the receiver will be stamped in their minds as a less-than-excellent prospect. Thus, if you do send a photocopied letter to several tailors, enclosing mailing costs is that much more advised. Once you're a regular, further samples should be expected gratis.

While it may seem risky dealing with firms halfway around the world, the establishments listed here have dealt with thousands of U.S. customers for years, establishing reputations spanning thousands of ocean miles. And a good reputation is a tailoring firm's most valuable asset. For in a word-of-mouth business, pleasing one client may bring in another three or four.

## Fabric Fancy

The main ingredient determining whether your custom-clothing creation is crème de la crème or something less appealing is its fabric. Whether visiting a tailor or ordering swatches through the mail, one guideline remains constant in choosing your garments' raw materials: Buy quality. Given good fabric, good Hong Kong tailors produce excellent wearables. Since the cost of fabric determines the cost of Orient-ordered clothes, it's tempting to cheap out on it.

Don't.

After all, you're going through the trouble of ordering custom (the initial groundwork for purchasing Hong Kong tailored garments is more strenuous than regular clothes shopping, although once it's in place reordering can be done from an armchair). So get the kind of fabric you'd have to pay the equivalent of a health club membership fee for in a ready-to-wear garment. This becomes all the more important when ordering conservative business wear. There's not much you can do with such clothing, style- and detail-wise. Fabric becomes its main aesthetic ingredient.

When you go shopping it seems easy to judge the quality of a fabric. You look at a garment's price tag (higher price, higher quality fabric). If you're a bit more informed, you twist a fistful of fabric in your hands to see if it wrinkles and how fast wrinkles fall out. Of the two methods, neither is surefire, and the second is probably as accurate as the first.

Judging the quality of swatches when you visit a tailor is just about as scientific, with few hard and fast rules. The price of the fabric should reflect its quality in relation to other fabrics of the same fiber and weight. And you can ball a swatch up, seeing if it wrinkles and how fast wrinkles fall out. The swatch also should have a marked vibrancy of color. And it should be soft and comfortable to the touch. Not coarse or harsh. Wools should have a slight sheen to their surfaces.

Ordering swatches by mail is obviously a bit tougher than picking from fabric swatch books in a hotel or Hong Kong showroom. You must communicate what fabrics you're interested in. Most guys are as well versed in the vocabulary of fabric weaves and weights as they are in Japanese flower arranging. But it's relatively easy to order fabric, especially with the guidelines given later in this chapter.

Still, if you don't want to mess with it you have three choices. You can describe in general terms what you're after. ("Please send swatches for a dark winter-weight business suit.") You can send a photograph of a garment made of the type of fabric you want. ("Please send me some sample swatches of fabric similar to that used in the shirt the man is wearing in this picture.") Or, if you own a garment made from the type of fabric you want, you can cut a small piece (a swatch of your own) from a hidden seam and send that along. ("Please send me sample swatches of suit fabric similar to the enclosed sample.")

Except for the last option, it's best to combine the above methods with a more exact description, one including the quality, composition, weight and color and pattern you're interested in. For example, a sample shirt-fabric description might be: "Please send me swatches of English Sea Island (quality—see below) cotton (composition) shirt fabrics (weight) in pale blues and white/navy stripes (color/ pattern). The following fabric "glossary" lists the most popular quality fabrics— remember, *always* quality—for custom-made shirts, pants and suits.

*SHIRTS.* For dress shirts English Sea Island cotton is considered champ. It's a medium-weight cloth of great durability and vibrancy. It washes up cleaner than a sanitized sink and resists wrinkles during wearing. The best Sea Island cotton (and all cottons) have a "high yarn count," meaning they incorporate more threads per square inch than other materials. However, high-count Sea Island shirting fabric is a luxury—it's hard to tell the difference from medium counts. For summer-weight dress or sport shirts, Swiss or French voile cottons and batiste weaves are as comfortable as shaded hammocks.

Silk shirts are a Hong Kong specialty seducing many an otherwise sober man. And why not? They have the eye appeal of lotus moons and are as inexpensive as an elegant piece of custom-fitted body sculpture can be. And an added plus: You can request hand-washable silk, saving enough on dry-cleaning bills to finance the shirt's purchase.

The most dressy silks are the Chinese crepes de chine (solid or patterned). This is the silk you probably think of when you think of silk—soft, shiny, elegant. But Hong Kong offers more silk possibilities than "one from column A, two from column B" combinations. For example, shantungs are slightly stiffer silks with interesting surface textures. Pongee silk is very flat surfaced and works well for dress shirts. Raw silk is heavy, with a nubby, sandy-looking surface; it might be used in one of your sport-shirt designs.

Of course, cottons and silks aren't the only shirt fabrics lining tailors' shelves. For example, cotton-and-polyester blends are well represented and inexpensively priced. The better blends are 55 percent cotton/45 percent polyester. If you're after easy-care wear or want to wager the smallest of sums on an Oriental apparel order, you'll find ordering shirts in cotton/poly blends a good bet.

The general rule on shirt fabrics: If you can communicate what you want, you'll get it in more patterns/colors than you've ever dreamed.

*PANTS.* Write saying you'd like swatches of pant fabrics in wool, wool/polyester, cotton, linen, etc., in light, medium or heavy weights. Since pant and suit fabrics are often the same, refer to the descriptions below for additional information.

*SUITS.* If you've never experienced the rather primal sartorial pleasure of picking from fifteen to twenty pinstripes or blues or glen plaids to determine which fabric you—not some designer—want to dress yourself in, you're in for an easily addictive experience. No more searching the racks of too-common clothing for something special. No more limited selections. There are literally hundreds of choices. It's a treat any clothing-conscious man should experience, and at Hong Kong prices it's treating yourself to a bargain.

The first fabric characteristic to consider: Do you want a suit (or pants or sport coat) in a light, medium or heavy weight? Lightweight, summer fabrics include seersucker, cotton poplin (especially in khaki shades), Italian silk suiting fabrics, Irish or Italian linen and blends of linen and silk or linen and cotton. An especially appealing summer-weight fabric is mohair. An elegant, high quality cloth, it's renowned for resisting and shedding wrinkles.

Medium-weight fabrics include wool and wool/polyester gabardine and 6–7 ounce worsted "tropical" wools, as well as a harbor full of various wool/polyester weaves.

For fall/winter-weight suits, 10–14 ounce English wool is the Sea Island cotton of suiting materials and very tough to beat. Because of the long British presence in Hong Kong, tailors there seem to have a broader variety than the Isles themselves. Some popular-weight wools include: flannel, usually in a range of grays but also available in blues; Harris Tweed, a texturally and visually intriguing fabric hand-woven from pure virgin wool, which is as hard wearing as a Scottish sea cliff; and worsted wools in a vast variety of colors, stripes and patterns, all with smooth, hard (and hard-wearing) finishes. Besides the traditional wools, such fabrics as

An all English-wool suit in a small herringbone pattern from Ying Tai, Ltd. Dress shirt sporting a "Prince Charles" collar from Sam's Tailor.

cashmere and cashmere/mink blends are available at a higher price.

*Note:* Fabric samples will come in the form of "swatch cards," usually including a dozen 1″ × 2″ fabric rectangles. Prices for a suit, pants, sport coat (or whatever you said you wanted) are usually printed, along with the numbers of the fabrics, somewhere on the card.

# Order Etiquette

You'll receive an order form along with your sample swatches. A rather intriguing document (it *looks* like a passkey to some exotic sartorial Shangri-la), it's the basic tool you'll use to communicate the style and measurements of your order. It will ask for your height, weight and age, as well as more body measurements than you thought you had. For example, Royal India Tailors' forms ask for twenty-one measurements, including jacket and topcoat length, chest, upper waist, waist, lower waist, hips, shoulders, sleeves and inseam. The form also contains several diagrams illustrating various body and shoulder "types." Drawings of the same figure in different postures include labels such as "Erect," "Extra Stout," "Extreme Hollow Back"; shoulder types are labeled "Sloping," "Regular," or "Square." It might be tempting to take your own measurements. But the task is best left to your local tailor, who should charge only a modest fee. (This man will no doubt try to dissuade you from your folly. Vested interest, you know. Hopefully, you're on a friendly enough basis for him to assent. If not, order forms illustrate where and how measurements should be taken.)

What makes possible mail ordering the Orient's custom clothes is Hong Kong tailors' renowned capacity to look at a set of body measurements and posture/shoulder descriptions, and visualize a man's physique. However, in practice it must be said that mistakes in sizing can and do occur from time to time. As Alan Flusser, a top American menswear designer who frequently travels to Hong Kong, puts it, "Making garments from a set of measurements is tricky business." Therefore, it's best to compensate for the lack of fittings by supplementing your order form's information—at least with suits (shirts and pants don't require it).

There are several methods for doing this. Seemingly cumbersome, they safeguard your order if you can't make it to Hong Kong or to a tailor's traveling rep (or if the tailor you choose doesn't have a traveling rep).

The method most recommended by Hong Kong tailors is to send a well-fitting garment of the type you want to be copied. It will be returned unharmed with your completed order. As mentioned, Hong Kong tailors beat Xerox for copying capability. But this doesn't mean losing the benefits of a better fit, unique styling or fabric choice. The garment you send is only used for measurements and for visualizing your shape (presumably it will have been altered to fit your physique's idiosyncracies). Your custom garment will fit better because it's an original piece of tailoring. And you can specify any problem areas in the garment you send. For example, you might send a suit, requesting that it be cut a little lower under the arms, not so tight around the rear and thighs, and fuller in the arms, making your custom version more comfortable than its prototype.

An alternative or addition to sending a garment is to send yourself, through

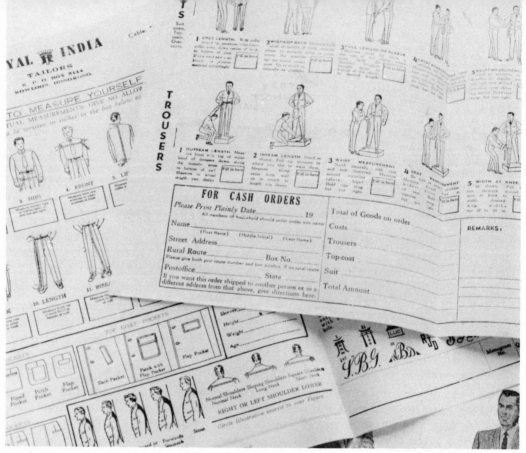

When requesting fabric swatches from Hong Kong tailors, you'll receive
an order form asking for your height, weight and age, as well as more
body measurements than you thought you had. Such forms are often
illustrated, showing how to have yourself measured.

photographs. When tailors come to the U.S. they often take a snapshot of a client in
his undershorts. This gives the stitcher back East (Far East, that is) a visual image to
go with the measurements. Obviously, if you have a Polaroid-type instant camera,
it's easy to do the same (one shot each of the front, side and back).

Fabric and fit aside, communicating the style and styling details of your order
isn't only essential but positively pleasurable. Unless you're sending a garment to
be copied exactly (or, if you've already had a suit made, reordering the same model
in a different fabric), pictures from magazines are the best way to communicate the
style you're after. To augment these, you can specify dimensions. For example, in
ordering a suit you might specify, 3¾"-wide notched lapels (most Hong Kong
tailors will give you 3¼" lapels if untutored), one 6"-long center vent in the jacket,
with 19½"-wide straight-leg, double-pleated trousers."

Order forms include spaces, often illustrated, for choosing such special styling details as the following:

| Detail | Variations |
|---|---|
| jacket pockets | : besom, flap, patch |
| pant pockets | : on seam, slanted, patch |
| pant-front finishing | : plain front, single pleats, double pleats |
| shirt collars | : cutaway, spread, button down, tab, etc. |
| shirt cuffs | : French, barrel |

Want more input into your individually minted wearables? Then exercise your freedom of choice. Designate the color and composition of jacket, suit and coat linings (rayon or silk, but you'll pay more for silk); thread color and composition (you might choose a contrasting white thread for a pair of black casual pants; silk thread is best, but again you'll have to pay a bit more); special inside jacket pockets for pens, pads, cigarettes, etc.; working sleeve button closures on jackets—touches making your custom crème de la crème clothing a combination of your imagination and your tailor's skill.

## Custom's Customs

Your wallet (meaning you, of course) will have to come up with customs duties on any Hong Kong apparel order sent from the Crown Colony. On some fabrics, particularly wool, these duties definitely dent your savings. But consider them the price of a bargain, because you're still getting a great one.

If your order is under $250 in value, the post office will collect the levies. If over that amount, you'll receive a Notice of Arrival when your goods come ashore. You'll then fill out formal entry papers, and may have to go to the airport to retrieve your clothes. If this is the case in your area of the country, you can avoid the process by telling your tailor to package your order in under-$250 parcels, billing you separately for each item.

You'll also have to pay postal charges from Hong Kong. You have a choice between air and sea shipping. Air mail is of course faster (one to three weeks as opposed to four to six), but twice as expensive (about $25 to air mail a two-piece wool suit, as opposed to $13 by sea). As of this writing some examples of customs duties on men's apparel were:

two-piece wool suits: 21 percent of value plus 35 cents per pound.
two-piece 35 percent wool/65 percent polyester suits: 27 percent of value plus 23 cents per pound.
wool pants: 21 percent of value plus 35 cents per pound.
cotton pants: 16.5 percent of value.
cotton shirts: 21 percent of value.
silk shirts: 14.6 percent of value.

# Shop Talking

Following is a list of Hong Kong tailors with long experience serving U.S. mail-order customers. What makes a good Hong Kong tailor? Workmanship is paramount. The tailors listed below pay their workmen more, and these employees in turn take more care in cutting and sewing your clothing. There are many shops in Hong Kong producing lower-priced clothes than the shops described here. They aren't worth a rubber shoelace. The prices quoted are approximations.

*Note:* You'll notice many of the establishments listed are headquartered in the Hotel Peninsula. This is because this is Hong Kong's grandest hotel/landmark. More Rolls-Royces pull up there per minute than at any other spot in Hong Kong. Thus to be at the Peninsula is equivalent to having your shop on Beverly Hills' Rodeo Drive or New York's 5th Avenue.

> YING TAI LIMITED
> Hotel Peninsula
> 1A, Mezzanine Floor
> Kowloon, Hong Kong

Originally founded in 1926, Ying Tai today boasts perhaps the largest list of top American executives and politicians who have suits done up in Hong Kong, as well as such celebrities as Steve Lawrence, Tom Jones and Andy Williams. Most of the shop's in-house tailors have over thirty years' experience, backed up by four small factories in Hong Kong.

The shop's specialty is what's best described as a "Hickey-Freeman replica." The kind of suit you expect to see on a Fortune 500 president, with smooth, rounded shoulders, a broad chest and conservative lapels and trousers (of course, Ying Tai can work up anything you have in mind).

The shop sends one of its most experienced tailors to the U.S. each year, equipped with close to a thousand fabric swatches. (Write to get on their mailing list; they'll send a note informing you when their man will be in or around your city.) You can also write for order forms and sample swatches.

Prices. Two-piece wool suits begin at $225, but better-quality wools start at $270–$280. For that price, you'll get a suit that stitch for stitch matches many of the best in the world. Pants start at $70. The firm doesn't make shirts, but winter coats are available, starting at $275. Once you've ordered, all Hong Kong tailors keep your measurements on file so reordering the same model garment is as easy as picking swatches. At Ying Tai, they make a paper pattern from a finished suit to store in your file.

*British classicism imbues a gray flannel suit from Sam's Tailor. Navy and white striped shirt in Sea Island cotton by Ascot Chang.*

SAM'S TAILOR
92-94 Nathan Road
Burlington Arcade "K"
Kowloon, Hong Kong

Sam's may well be the most famous tailoring shop in the world. It seems to have a faculty for attracting traveling statesmen. President Ford, Henry Kissinger, Alexander Haig and a number of English noblemen, including Prince Charles himself, are said to frequent Sam's when in Hong Kong. (Such a royal clientele created a sartorial storm several years ago; some British garment unions became incensed upon learning that the Textile Minister, H.R.H. the Duke of Kent, had some suits sewn up at Sam's—eschewing London's best establishments.) Another distinction: The shop has been documented as holding the world record for making a three-piece custom suit—two hours, six minutes flat, from first measuring to final fitting.

The shop's specialty is an English-cut "Prince Charles" suit. This is a shaped garment, with an "hourglass" silhouette—slightly padded but natural-looking shoulders, broad chest, slim waist, straight-leg trousers—the most classic of classic suits. (Again, this doesn't preclude other styles—they'll produce whatever you want.)

Prices. Two-piece wool suits start at $150. Shirts: polyester/cotton, $15–$25; cotton, $15–$50; silk, $20–$50 (request pearl buttons or you'll get plastic). Pants: $40–$100. Sam's prices are so reasonable for two reasons. One, he owns his own shop and factory spaces, allowing him to avoid high Hong Kong rents. Two, he services a broad clientele, from the polyester set to the no-holds-barred cashmere crowd.

And that's the rub.

The shop employs over forty tailors of varying skill levels. To get the shop's best work you have to ask—and pay—for it. This involves choosing a top fabric and requesting that a top cutter and sewer be assigned your order. You can even ask for M. (for middle son) Sam, the shop's manager, to cut it himself. Sam's *can* turn out suits costing four times the price on Savile Row, but these suits start in the $275 range. (At the time of this writing Sam's was considering sending an annual envoy to the U.S. to take orders.)

T. M. Tom
Hotel Peninsula
8, Mezzanine Floor
Kowloon, Hong Kong

T. M. Tom is another of Hong Kong's top tailors sending a representative to major U.S. cities each year. The shop prides itself on turning out suits with the latest European styling and on being able to copy to the last stitch any suit you send. Thus, if you're after, say, a very Italian look to your garments, Tom can deliver it at bargain rates.

Prices. Two-piece wool suits start at $220 (wool/poly, $195). Shirts: cotton, $45 and up; silk, $55 and up. Pants: $65 and up.

Henry The Tailor
17 Cameroon Road, 2nd Floor
Kowloon, Hong Kong

Henry The Tailor's clients talk of the shop in tones reserved for old, dear friends. And the small, dark abode has been making lifelong friends for over twenty years. Perhaps because, as Henry's daughter puts it, "We try our best to do the best we can."

And that happens to be very good. The firm uses all-English materials, except for Chinese silks for shirts and some Italian silks for suits—sure signs of a quality operation. As of this writing, the shop was preparing to send a tailor to the U.S. for order taking.

Prices. Two-piece wool suits start at $240. Shirts: cotton/polyester, $20; cotton, $24 and up; silk, $40 and up. Pants: $55 and up.

ROYAL INDIA TAILORS
51-52 Haiphong Road, 9th Floor
Kowloon, Hong Kong
U.S. Representative:
SHANGHAI CUSTOM TAILORS
500 North Michigan Avenue, Suite 540
Chicago, IL 60611   Tel: 312-527-0395

Founded fifty years ago, Royal India is a family business continuing to thrive, offering U.S. customers a permanent stateside representative. There are several advantages to this. One, since you buy your suit from the Chicago-based Shanghai Custom Tailors, you don't have to pay customs duties (these are paid on the wholesale price of your garments by the stateside firm). Two, Shanghai Custom has a salesman on the road fifteen days out of every month, who is able to service smaller cities than the once-a-year reps from other Hong Kong firms limit themselves to.

Prices are extremely low, but this is a case of getting what you pay for, as the workmanship may not be on the same level as the other firms listed here. (However, if something is wrong with a garment, it's relatively easy for the Chicago-based firm to remedy it.)

Prices. Two-piece wool suits start at $195 (wool/poly, $175). Shirts: cotton, $13.50–$20; silk, $35–60. Pants: $35 and up.

ASCOT CHANG
Hotel Peninsula
6, Mezzanine Floor
Kowloon, Hong Kong

In business over forty years and serving over 10,000 worldwide customers, Ascot Chang is the Crown Colony's premiere shirtmaker. The company sends a representative to the U.S. each year to take orders, and his suitcases bulge with dozens and dozens of sample swatch books.

You can also request order forms and sample swatches, and there's no charge for the ample variety you'll receive. (While the number of swatches sent depends on the fabric you're interested in, you may receive as many as fifty). With more than 2,500 shirting fabrics on hand, the firm can out-duel your imagination when it comes to coming up with top tops. As to shirt collars, a whopping twenty-three styles are available for your perusal.

Prices. English Sea Island cotton and French and Swiss voile, $35–$45; Chinese crepes de chine, $50; Chinese silk shantung, $40; pongee silk, $40. White cuffs and collars on colored shirts are $4 extra. Monograms, $2 extra. All shirts come with pearl buttons, and any design details are included at no extra charge (a shirt with two pockets costs the same as the same shirt without pockets).

LEE KUNG MAN KNITTING FACTORY
77 Wing Lok Street
Central District, Hong Kong

This shop has gained a worldwide reputation for, of all things, its unparalleled men's T-shirts. (No, they're not custom made, but it's good to know of them, isn't it?) About $10 buys the world's finest all-cotton shirt in short- or long-sleeve models. The cloth is 120-count English yarn. That's about six times as dense a cotton weave as standard American-made varieties. The shirts are virtually shrink free; however, the largest size is 42. The company also makes an excellent long-sleeve wool T-shirt costing about $25, also of the highest quality. *Note:* Prices are approximate. Write for current prices and shipping charges.

## · 4 ·

# LONG-DISTANCE DIRECT

## Mail-Order Shopping
## to Save

SAVING'S GRACES are only a postage stamp away.

Addressing the realm of mail-order bargains, you can deliver yourself cut-rate prices from your easy chair (or couch, waterbed or porch swing, for that matter). Using catalogues, bargain hunting becomes about as tough a task as scanning the newspaper's sports section. Why search for deals on duds? Let them come to you.

## Ways and Means

Not all mail-order clothing operations offer garments for less, of course, but many do, through a variety of means. One is by manufacturing what they sell. "We manufacture almost everything that goes into our catalogue. We've eliminated the middleman, and as a result we've been able to offer items of a very high quality level, but at a much lower price," explained a spokesperson for Britches of Georgetowne, which sends out thousands of "Everything Britches" catalogues twice a year. "For example, we sell a beautiful wool navy blazer for about $145. And you couldn't touch its quality for under $200 in most stores." (*Note:* The addresses of firms mentioned in this chapter can be found in the chapter's mail-order directory, "Selective Reading". For mail-order firms not included in the directory, addresses are provided as the companies are mentioned.)

On one end of the mail-order manufacturing spectrum are firms like Britches, utilizing warehouse loads of fabric in their custom designs. But some of the most intriguing mail-order shopping opportunities are products of much smaller operations. For example, a ranch operation raising its own sheep and spinning its own wool for use in hand-knit sweaters sold only by mail, or a boxing-equipment manufacturer turning out small quantities of floor-length terry cloth robes for $20.

Sometimes mail-order houses can offer you low prices because of their minimal overhead. Sure, they often pay shipping and handling costs. But they may be located in a neck of the woods far removed from high store rents and property taxes. For example, a small shop shipping warm-up suits from the outskirts of Wichita, Kansas, isn't footing the city-slicker bills of downtown men's shops in, say, Chicago or Houston.

Also, many by-mail businesses keep clothing prices at ground level through volume orders. For example, L. L. Bean, a mail-order house that has become an American institution, mails over 9 million catalogues a year, garnering over $150 million worth of orders.

And there are downward price pressures apart from self-made goods, low overhead and volume orders. Built into store-to-door buying are tangible and intangible money savers. A tangible: When ordering from an out-of-state firm you skip paying sales taxes (unless the outfit operates a branch office in your state). Another tangible: You save money on gas or public transportation. This may sound piddling, but any distance you drive means paying a gas tax on your store-bought clothes. Finally, an intangible: time. Admittedly, store shopping can be fun. But if you're the type who prefers to enter a store, get what you need and exit post haste, the time savings mail ordering affords is considerable.

## Postal Purchasing Perks

You can't tag a price to some shopping-by-the-book advantages. For example, how much is it worth to have goods unavailable in your city delivered to your doorstep? It would be very valuable if you were, say, a Detroit resident planning a trip to Hawaii in November. Where to get some tropical togs? By mail, of course.

And the hassle-free aspect of shopping by mail is worth a lot to some guys. (Yes, there can be problems. But you're going to learn how to avoid/deal with them.) A lot of men just don't like shopping, period. With mail order you shop when you want. Armed with catalogues, you can pick ten items in ten days, ten months or ten minutes. And after you're on a mailing list, new books usually arrive each fall and spring. There are no crowds, rude sales help or checkout lines when buying by mail, and unlike in some stores, you're frequently offered the advantages of a trial period and an exchange/refund guarantee.

Ironically, some catalogues even proffer more specific, practical information about the clothes you're buying than store sales help. For example, in a recent "Everything Britches" catalogue a JanSport Diamond Ski Coat, made of the synthetic material Gore-Tex, was introduced by this information:

> Gore-Tex. For years outdoorsmen could get wet in either of two ways. They could choose waterproof clothing that kept out the rain but left uncomfortable body moisture in, or breathable clothing that let out body moisture but left them soaked from the rain. Gore-Tex fabric, with over 9 billion pores per square inch, is an incredible new material that keeps you dry from the inside and out. Rain can't get in, because each pore is 20,000 times smaller than a drop of water. Those same pores, however, are 700 times larger than a molecule of water vapor, and that allows body moisture to escape. Lightweight, functional Gore-Tex fabrics make breathable, waterproof outerwear a reality.

Of course, not all catalogue entries are treatise length. For example, a suit description from a recent Brooks Brothers catalogue reads: "Trim 2-button worsted herringbone suit for the Brooksgate young executive in dark brown or grey. Coat, vest and trousers." (Apparently, Brooks Brothers customers need know little else.)

Still another advantage to postal purchasing: You can compare prices on some types of garments at home. Looking to order a sweater, ski jacket, walking shorts or chino trousers? You can compare specifications and prices on a dozen models in your living room.

## Pages of Plenty

Mining mail order's cache of clothing can load your wardrobe with rich wearables. The finds are abundant, ranging from cashmere sweaters, rugby jerseys, soccer shorts, oxford cloth shirts, regimental striped ties, leather flight jackets, woven leather belts, cords and jeans, cotton sweaters, wash-and-wear suits and porkpie hats, to chino pants, polo shirts, lambswool sweater vests, khaki trail shorts, olive drab briefs, nylon parkas, racing swim suits, hiking and cowboy boots, tennis shoes, jogging outfits and T-shirts.

But while the range of catalogue-carried garments is as wide as the smile of the late Leon Leonwood Bean up in mail-order heaven, there are several categories of catalogues currently predominating in the mails. Of the mail-order books featuring clothing, by far the largest lot are those of, as L. L. Bean's catalogue puts it, "Outdoor Sporting Specialists." While Bean's is the most popular, there's a national park full of imitators. Most revel in the homey, folksy images we tend to associate with "outdoor people."

The popularity of such outdoorsy "books" (as those in the mail-order business sometimes term catalogues) prompted a writing team, William Dasheff and Laura Dearborn, to compile a book featuring the clothing they tend to stock. Entitled

*Value-priced sweaters
are in plentiful supply
from "outdoorsy" catalogues.*

*Good Garb* (New York: Dell Publishing, 1980. $9.95), it lists more than thirty mail-order sources offering such apparel. The authors aptly describe the appeal this clothing holds for many when they write: "These clothes offer a rational and constructive alternative to the tiresome and wasteful gimmickry of conventional fashion. The emphasis here is on utility, durability, effectiveness of design, ease of maintenance, and timeless styling." Of course, each of the Bean-type books offers a homespun twist on the theme. And most emphasize either hunting, fishing or camping, with many of their pages devoted to outdoor equipment and supplies.

Another mail room full of product presenters is aimed at the guy who, on weekends, L. L. Bean catalogue tucked in canvas knapsack, hikes through wooded dales, fishes in rock-bedded, icy streams, and camps wherever his Jeep takes him, then comes back into town during the week to hold down the most conservative of corporate positions. (Do these people really exist? If they don't, there are a lot of pretenders out there.)

*A variety of parkas and other outdoor wearables are available through the mails.*

Brooks Brothers is the Bean's of this field. Others include Chipp, Inc. (14 East 44th Street, New York, NY 10017), F. R. Tripler (366 Madison Avenue, New York, NY 10017), and Dunham's of Maine (33 College Avenue, Waterville, ME 04901. Catalogue: $1). With a more sophisticated eye, but appealing to the same type of solid individuals, are such firms as Cable Car Clothiers, Britches of Georgetowne, and Paul Stuart (Madison Avenue at 45th Street, New York, NY 10017. Catalogue: $2.50).

Another batch of clothes/equipment sellers purveying goods through print are the leather-necked military surplus outfits such as Brigade Quartermasters. The book's descriptive copy is as smooth and polished as raw granite, its photographs as slick as dried beef. Ditto the items presented.

Comprising a catalogue category growing by leaps, bounds, laps and marathons are publications proffering active sportswear. An example is from The Finals, a brochure sporting healthy discounts on every page, sent through the mails

*One category of catalogues growing by leaps, bounds, laps and marathons is publications doling out active sportswear.*

by a swimwear/activewear manufacturer offering "factory-direct" prices. And more direct-to-you fitness-wear firms are sending their offerings sprinting off the presses every year.

Most mail-order clothing catalogues fit into one of the above categories. But sliding into mail slots next to them are brochures, pamphlets and price lists from firms with specialized visions. Some absolutely itching to ship you a bargain.

Literally dozens of catalogues containing clothing are being published. Not all offer great prices. But some will lick your high wardrobe costs if you'll only give them a stamp of approval.

## Write to Conquer

Your first move in implementing a money-saving mail-order strategy will be collecting a set of catalogues, a library for researching cost-conscious clothing finds. These mailings will vary in look. Some will be as lushly produced as the finest magazines, with professional models posed on glossy color pages. Others will have the glossy pages, but, as in Bean's and many other outdoor-oriented books, the firm's employees will don the clothes for photographs. (A practice resulting in some corny but true-to-life presentations.) Still others will be photocopies of typed price lists.

Firms usually publish their catalogues twice yearly (although many mail special Christmas editions, too). These start filling mailmen's pouches in August and September for the fall season, in January and February for spring. You'll find a source guide to publications listing catalogues at the end of this chapter, and you're sure to spot many ads for them in your favorite magazines.

Before the advent of high paper and printing costs, many catalogues were free. Some still are. But the majority will put you out a dollar or two, with this cost often being credited toward your first order.

When sending for catalogues that cost, send the required sum with your request letter. If the amount is less than $1, tape coins to a three-by-five-inch card for mailing. Dollar bills should be folded before being slipped into an envelope. If over $1, use a check or money order. In your note asking for a publication, write your return address clearly and include the date, and since some houses publish more than one catalogue, state the specific one you're interested in. If enclosing money, tell them how much you've sent. The envelope your note goes in should also carry your return address, and you might get faster service by jotting "Catalogue Request" under the firm's address. (*Note:* Sometimes a company publishing price lists will ask for a self-addressed, stamped envelope. If so, use a #10 (business) size envelope, including it with your request.)

Your library of clothing bargains will start shaping up two to four weeks after your initial round of requests. However, in January, and again in July and August, some companies are between seasons and will wait to send you their latest offering. The request process may be a one-time affair. Once you're on a company's mailing list you'll usually receive free catalogues for several seasons.

## Picture Perfect

If you've never ordered clothing by mail you probably have some doubts about it. Don't you have to try clothes on before you buy? Can you really get a good fit? How can you pick another color from the one shown in the catalogue?

If your physique boasts extra inches here or odd curves there, you may encounter roadblocks to correct fitting in certain garments (in tailored suits, sport coats and overcoats, for example). But most wearables offered by mail aren't tailored (knitted shirts and sweaters, active sportswear, parkas, socks, shorts and ponchos, for example). So even if you're odd, size-wise, a small, medium, large or extra-large will likely hang your way, just as in store shopping.

And an ordered garment *beats* that encountered on many store shelves for size and selection. For example, many shirts in stores come with sleeves in 32–33 or

34–35 inch lengths. On similar mail-ordered shirts, exact sleeve lengths are to be had. Pants are often shipped finished to your correct inseam length, saving you tailoring charges.

How many times has this story unfolded? You spot a pant style you like in a store, only to find your size not available? That can happen but usually doesn't when shopping through your mailbox.

As for picking colors from a photograph or a description such as "sailor's blue," well, there's no denying it's not an exact science. Searching for a precise color is best done in stores. If the garment's design is your primary consideration, however, and the color a classic (khaki, navy blue, light blue, white, forest green, scarlet red and wine come to mind) you won't have trouble homing in on the right hue by mail.

The bottom line on fantastic fits and correct colors by mail: If you don't like what you get, send it back for a refund or exchange. Simple as that.

## Order Easy

You receive your catalogues. You peruse their pages. And damned if you don't find a number of suitable garments, clothes seemingly poised on their pages in readiness, eager to enliven your sartorial style *and* save you a wad of dough in the process. It's time to order.

But first, check to see that there's a "satisfaction guaranteed" provision. The term, coined in the 1800s by Montgomery Ward to reassure their rural customers, is still your best bet for getting goods as they're described. If there's not some sort of guarantee, shop elsewhere. If, instead of ordering soon after your books arrive, you let them lie for a while, check their date. If a catalogue is six months old or older, write for the latest issue. (Or, if the firm has a toll-free number, call to check if the clothing you want is still stocked, and if prices have changed.)

Now find the book's order blank. Before filling it out, check it for special offers such as a free T-shirt with every $20 order or, more likely, a minimum order requirement. Besides spaces for model numbers, colors and quantities, order forms may have sections for shipping, insurance, handling and sales tax charges. Many firms include the first three in the item's price, but if you're responsible, here's a rundown on these small expenses.

Some shipping charges are based on weight, some on price. If weight is used, the weight of your garments will be printed beside their prices or order numbers. Sometimes maps divided by zones will be printed on order forms, leaving you to calculate postage due for each price category.

Firms usually pick up the tab for insurance. It's a nonexistent or negligible expense, as most use United Parcel Service (UPS) delivery, and UPS automatically insures each parcel to $100. The company charges about 25 cents for each extra $100 in value, and this is the fee you sometimes must pay. *Note:* If you know you won't be home during the day, when UPS delivers, have orders sent to where you work.

Handling charges, covering boxes, wrapping, etc., plus the labor involved in packing your clothes for their journey, are costs passed on to you by the firm. Again, if you're charged it won't be a bank breaker. As mentioned, don't pay sales tax if ordering out-of-state, unless the catalogue lists a branch office in your home state.

Order blank penned in, check it over; the most common mail-ordering mistake is filling out order forms incorrectly. ("What's this? *I* didn't order elephant-skin underwear. . . .") And the most common faux pas on order forms is inverted numbers, so check their sequences.

Now comes money time. Order forms will tell you how many ways the firm will take your cash. Actually, *never send cash.* Use one of four payment plans: personal checks, money orders, charge cards or Cash on Delivery (C.O.D.).

Personal checks are convenient and inexpensive and can give you an easy-to-work-with record proving you paid. A hitch: Some companies don't process orders until checks clear, which results in a one to two week lapse in the time it takes to get the goods. On the other hand, money orders are treated as cleared checks by firms. They can be bought from your bank or post office, the small fee determined by the order's dollar amount.

Nothing could be easier than using charge cards to order your clothes by phone. This wave-of-the-future idea is already the most popular form of catalogue order payment. No order forms or stamps, no writing, a few flicks of the ol' fingers and you start the clothes coming. Many firms, perhaps as many as 50 percent of them, have set up toll-free 800 numbers for you to call. (For example, during the Christmas season L. L. Bean employs over twenty phone operators to handle incoming orders.)

With card and catalogue in hand you call, tell what you want, and soon the object of your desire is wheeling or flying your way. To make sure you're using a card belonging to you, you may be asked to give certain verifiable information such as your bank, where you work and home phone number.

C.O.D. shipments involve some form of later-day payment for your by-mail wearables. This may include shipping costs, balance due on an item (if you've paid a deposit), or the full amount of your merchandise, plus shipping costs. Potential problems with C.O.D.: You must pay the UPS driver or the mailman whatever is due on your goods, plus the small C.O.D. delivery fee, with cash or a certified check.

# Return to Sender

What if what you saw isn't what you get? What if the clothes you receive don't meet your expectations or don't fit? Exchanges and refunds are no problem.

If, that is, you checked before ordering to make sure the company accepts them. Nearly all do, as they want satisfied, eager-to-reorder customers.

Many firms have guarantees similar to L. L. Bean's "100 percent Guarantee," which states, "All our products are guaranteed to be 100 percent satisfactory. Return anything purchased from us that proves otherwise. We will replace it, refund your money, or credit your charge card." *Note:* Most companies appreciate your using the original boxes and packing when returning items. While returns are easy to implement, your mail-order return rate will probably be about the same as to stores you shop in person. Most mail-ordered bargains slip into your sartorial sync right out of the box.

# Selective Reading

Following is a list of catalogues offering bargain buys. It's far from complete, highlighting only some of the ready-to-be-shipped selections your mailbox-as-savings-source can produce. All prices are approximate.

BAKER STREET SHIRTMAKERS
281 Centennial Avenue
Piscataway, NJ 08854
800-526-3941

Baker Street Shirtmakers, a direct-to-the-public division of the 124-year-old Van Heusen shirt company, delivers a catalogue of straightforward, priced-right shirts in classic patterns and colors. Shirts are in a regular cut, described as "full but not tentlike." Some sample items:

> Solid, striped and checked oxford cloth button-down dress shirts in cotton/polyester, about $18.
> 100 percent cotton seersucker sport shirts with two button-through chest pockets, about $16.

BANANA REPUBLIC
410 Townsend Street
Box 77133/San Francisco, CA 94107
415-777-5200   Catalogue: $1.

This little mailer has the look of an anthropologist's notebook. (It's labeled, "Authentic Safari Travel Clothes for Men and Women.") Garments are drawn in

*Specialized clothing sources such as Banana Republic, billing itself as a supplier of "Authentic Safari & Travel Clothes for Men and Women," make shopping by mail an adventure.*

exact detail, as if they were unearthed discoveries that have been, well, catalogued for later study back at camp. Many items are so quality soaked they must carry heady price tags. But some equally durable and natty numbers—mostly military surplus goods from around the world—are priced to please even the most frugal explorers of the sartorial jungle. Some sample items of the type usually stockpiled (although these particular items may no longer be available when you get your catalogue):

"Authentic British Drill Trousers" are made of 100 percent cotton drill cloth in a khaki color. The vintage trousers sport an adjustable waist wrap and deep pleats. About $30.

"Authentic Australian Bush Shorts" are long, reaching the knees. Produced in Australia in the 1940s of 100 percent cotton twill, they're in a "moss-tinted khaki" color. Their description notes: "We discovered the shorts stockpiled in Sydney." About $16.

"Hooded bush vests" are equipped with "back pockets, front pockets, side pockets, bellows pockets, hidden pockets, eight in all. Deep, long, compact, roomy pockets." About $40.

Jos. A. Bank Clothiers
109 Market Place
Baltimore, MD 21202
301-937-8838

Traditional business wear and classic casual attire, with a dress-for-success look impregnated in every pinstripe and button-down collar—all of it priced 20 to 30 percent below comparable department store merchandise. Bank does it by manufacturing most of what it sells. Result: dozens upon dozens of garments (over forty-five suit models alone) fashioned for journeys up the corporate ladder, at prices someone starting in the mail room could afford. Some sample items:

100 percent worsted-wool two-piece suits, about $175.
Two-piece mid-wale corduroy suits, about $140.
Tan gabardine trench coats with zip-out wool-and-nylon liners and insulated sleeves, about $165.
Topcoats of 70 percent cashmere, 15 percent wool and 15 percent nylon, about $220.
100 percent cotton oxford cloth shirts, about $20.
100 percent silk ties in dozens of stripes, paisley and foulard designs, about $13.50.

L. L. Bean, Inc.
Freeport, ME 04033
207-865-3111

The world's most successful, most imitated mail-order catalogue should be the first you order. One, because it's free. Two, because it contains the lowest prices on many basic garments sold by a number of mail-order firms. Three, because Bean's has a reputation for service that's unparalleled. Some sample items:

Soft, three-ply Ragg wool crew neck sweaters, about $19.75.
100 percent oxford cloth button-downs, about $17.
100 percent cotton "Double L" polo shirts, about $13.75.
Suede Sports Caps of brushed pigskin, about $11.

*L. L. Bean's clothing is traditional in orientation, value priced and extremely serviceable.*

BENCONE UNIFORMS
121 Carver Avenue
Westwood, NJ 07675
800-631-4602
Uniforms, including Operating Room smocks and chef's coats. See chapter 11.

BRIGADE QUARTERMASTERS, LTD.
266 Roswell Street
Marietta, GA 30060
404-428-1234   Catalogue: $2.

Here's a rough 'n' ready, no-nonsense book billed as, "Goods for survival, camping, hunting and military." The photographs are straightforward. The descriptive copy long on specific details, short on glamor. Lots of military gear, much of it in olive, khaki and camouflage fabrics. *Plus* some of the grimmest-looking military/outdoor boots around. Some sample items:

Camouflage T-shirts with short sleeves (about $7.50) or long (about $10.50).
Authentic "U.S.M.C. Camo [for camouflage] Utilities." About $26. "Woodland Pattern Jungle Fatigues." About $24.
Military khaki trousers of 100 percent cotton twill. About $21.
And, as the catalogue puts it: "P.X. Permanent-Press O.D. Fatigues. P.X. contract stock to specification. Army approved. Olive Green 507 shade. 50 percent polyester/50 percent cotton." About $16.

BRITCHES OF GEORGETOWNE
1321 Leslie Avenue
Alexandria, VA 22301
703-548-0200
800-336-5041

The most handsome menswear catalogue published, bar none. And because Britches manufactures most of the items it contains, prices are kept comparatively low. Some sample items:

A double-breasted trench coat includes a removable wool lining. About $165.
A unique feature of the Britches catalogue is the excellent descriptive copy accompanying its offerings. For example, a wool navy blazer's presentation is supplemented by the following information:
The navy blazer. Late one evening, after a particularly lengthy and grueling deployment, the H.M.S. *Blazer* came home to port. The captain of this mid-1860s English vessel, noting that his crew was a disreputable-looking lot, ordered them all to wear dark blue jackets with metal British Navy buttons. Their appearance was so dramatically improved that the Blazer, despite slight modifications to its original nautical style, today remains a symbol of dignity.
Britches' own traditionally distinctive model sells for about $145.

BROOKS BROTHERS
346 Madison Avenue
New York, NY 10017
800-247-1000
Catalogue: sample copy free; $2 for a 12-month subscription

Many of the items in the regular Brooks Brothers catalogue are had from the venerable firm's imitators for less money. For example, Brooks's Scottish wool tweed herringbone sport jacket runs about $300.

However, toward the back of the company's book, and in a separate, smaller publication, is the Brooksgate selection, described as "for the young executive who wants up-to-date clothing and furnishings with the assurance of Brooks Brothers taste and quality." Here's where your bargains are. Most are made by Brooks Brothers in their own factory. Virtually everything in the separate Brooksgate catalogue is a good bet—inexpensive, with the type of styling you can wear from now until retirement. Some sample items:

> Long-sleeved oxford cloth shirts with white broadcloth collars, about $23.
> Wool tweed herringbone "odd jackets" (sport coats), about $155.
> Worsted all-wool tweed herringbone vested suits, about $215.
> Wool and mohair knit ties, about $11.
> Etc., etc., all with the Brooks stamp.

CABELA'S
812 13th Avenue
Sidney, NE 69162
308-254-5505

At a glance the Cabela's catalogue could be mistaken for an issue of *Outdoor Life*, with its cover of a hooked trout snapping out of the water, colorful fishing lure dangling from its jaws. About 75 percent of the magazine-sized mail-order trove is devoted to fishing and hunting equipment. But the remaining pages offer wearables for beefing up your casual clothing wardrobe. Some sample items:

> Cotton/polyester polo shirts with the company's own embroidered fish-on-the-line chest emblem. About $13.
> 100 percent cotton pullover sweaters patterned after "the original WWII fatigue issue sweater." The pullover's main detail: a collar that can be buttoned right up to the chin for extra warmth. About $19.
> Nylon jackets feature an outer shell of water-repellent nylon with a lining of soft 100 percent cotton chamois cloth. With drawstring waist, snap front and knit wrists. About $27.

CABLE CAR CLOTHIERS
Robert Kirk, Ltd.
No. 150, Post Street
San Francisco, CA 94108
415-397-7733

Cable Car bills itself as "San Francisco's British Goods Store Since 1939." Scanning the catalogue can be frustrating. If only the prices were lower! If the costs of the obviously high quality, tasteful as a top hat clothing were a third less, this would be the catalogue to have if you could only have one. However, the upper-crust operation does seem to pride itself on the price of its wash-and-wear wool/ Dacron and cotton/Dacron suits.

One model's description:

> Cable Car/Robert Kirk's classic poplin suit tailored in a cool, washable blend of cotton and Dacron. Excellent for business or travel in any season, but especially comfortable in warmer weather. Easy-fitting, soft natural shoulder, 3-button model with patch and flap pockets, welted edges. Jacket and trousers also double as separates. In versatile colours of tan, navy or olive. About $165.

CAMP BEVERLY HILLS
9615 Brighton Way
Beverly Hills, CA 90210
213-202-0069   Catalogue: $1

Active sportswear for a "no-sweat" look. See chapter 10.

COACH LEATHERWARE/COACH CONSUMER SERVICE
516 West 34th Street
New York, NY 10001
212-594-3914

Coach leather goods have a deservedly high reputation for the kind of quality and durability that make them possible generation-to-generation hand-me-downs. But, surprisingly, their men's belts seem inexpensive. After all, their leather is tanned to soft-but-indestructible perfection, and only the best solid brass hardware ("each buckle cast in sand") latches it together. Some sample items:

> 1-inch wide tab belt of "especially supple, self-lined, glove leather," about $27.
> 1-inch wide bridle belt of glove-tanned cowhide, outfitted with a square-cornered buckle polished to mirror brightness, about $22.
> Striped wool fabric belts with leather/brass hardware, about $17.

COLONEL BUBBIE'S/STRAND SURPLUS SENTER (sic)
2202 Strand
Galveston, TX 77550
713-762-7397   Catalogue: $1

An ever-shifting list of military surplus goods. Including highly serviceable wear from military forces around the world. Some sample items from a recent list:

> Used 100 percent cotton "genuine Dutch Army" pleated paratrooper pants. In gray chino cloth, featuring five pockets. About $14.
> 100 percent cotton Spanish Air Force utility jackets, endowed with two pockets and a knit waist and cuffs. About $25.

EASTERN MOUNTAIN SPORTS, INC.
One Vose Farm Road
Peterborough, NH 03458
603-924-9571
800-343-9700

This mail-order source offers all the L. L. Bean-type requisites: Ragg wool sweaters, chamois cloth shirts, canvas pants, hiking shorts, etc. However, styles are updated, with a younger cut, and thus Eastern Mountain's higher prices may be justified. Some sample items:

> The EMS Flannel Shirt, made exclusively for the company, carries this description: "The traditional way to keep warm on a chilly day. Soft, comfortable, 100

percent yarn-dyed cotton in traditional tartan plaids. Very handsome, with long sleeves, long tails, and two button-down pockets. Great value." And it is, at about $19.

At the back of the book, amongst the Pauligk nuts, carabiners and other professional mountain climbing equipment: "climber's belts," of 1 inch nylon webbing. In bright colors, about $4.50.

EASTERN WEAR-GUARD
P.O. Box 239
Cambridge, MA 02141
617-871-4100
800-343-4406
Uniform/work wear at low prices. See chapter 11.

THE FINALS
21 Minisink Avenue
Port Jervis, NY 12771
914-856-4456
800-431-9111
Swimwear/active sportswear savings. See chapter 10.

*A swim cap for*
*a buck fifty?*
*Only through the mails.*

FRENCH CREEK SHEEP AND WOOL CO.
Route No. 1
Elverson, PA 19520
215-286-5700
800-345-4091

French Creek's merchandise isn't cheap, but it certainly is inexpensive. That is, the firm's distinctive, bulky hand-loomed sweaters offer the kind of quality you'd have to pay twice as much for in better department stores. And it's hard not to like the operation: The company runs a cottage industry nestled amongst the green hills in Pennsylvania Dutch country. Local knitters, many older women, use hand-operated flatbed machines to knit sweater panels to shape (rather than the mass-produced cut-and-sewn variety). Some sample collectibles:

Hand-framed and hand-sewn all-cotton sweaters "produced by the ladies of French Creek in their own homes." About $60.
Shawl-collared, bulky wool cardigans with hand-sewn buttonholes and woven leather buttons. About $150.

GANDER MOUNTAIN, INC.
P.O. Box 248, Highway W
Wilmot, WI 53192
414-862-2331
800-558-9410

Another outdoor/hunting catalogue. Ho. Hum.

But wait! There are some *values* tucked between the Bowie knives and $350 crossbows. Take a Gander at these sample items:

Quilt-lined shirts, featuring cotton flannel shells with a quilted polyester-filled lining. About $20.

Flannel-lined khaki pants show tough cotton/polyester twill to a cold world, while a soft flannel lining warms your legs. About $21.

Quoting the catalogue on Gander's quilted chamois cloth vest: "Such a practical and good-looking idea we're surprised no one has thought of it before." Us, too. The vest sports heavyweight (10 oz.) chamois cloth outside, quilted insulation inside. About $18.

G & S SPORTING GOODS
43 Essex Street
New York, NY 10002
212-777-7590

Boxing gear and active sportswear at knockout prices. See chapter 10.

INTERNATIONAL MALE
Box 85043
2802 Midway Drive
San Diego, CA 92138
619-226-8751   Catalogue: $2

This is a men's fashion catalogue laid out in the style of *Gentlemen's Quarterly*, the men's fashion magazine. The mailer has its own question-and-answer column, "Dressing Right," and, like most fashion magazine layouts, its photographs are shot on location using professional-looking models. To complete the catalogue-as-magazine approach, I.M. carries advertisements from manufacturers!

The firm manufactures much of its own active sportswear, which is as Californian in its orientation as The Beach Boys. The catalogue also includes offerings from name European and American designers. Bargains, however, in the sense of inexpensive items that are obviously priced below normal levels, are hard to come by. Some sample items:

A white canvas summer jacket, about $55.

Canvas swimsuit, about $18.

From a full line of "fashion underwear," a pair of silk briefs, about $13.

*Special wardrobe additives like silk*
*underwear are easily mail ordered.*

H. Kauffman & Sons Saddlery Co., Inc.
139–141 East 24th Street
New York, NY 10010
212-684-6060   Catalogue: $2
This is the "complete illustrated guide to English and Western boots, saddles, riding clothes, books, gifts and equipment." And if you don't own a pony 90 percent of its contents will be as useful to you as flight reservations to Mars. Still, the belts (starting at $12) have the last-longer-than-your-current-waistline look to them, and the authentic Western shirts (from under $25) are, well, authentic.

Kreeger & Sons
16 West 46th Street
New York, NY 10036
212-575-7825
This plummy little catalogue is chock-full of down-home, friendly talk. And

more important, friendly prices on what the company terms "basics." In their own words: "What we are today is a company that offers the basics [in clothing] to people who appreciate quality and value." Some sample items:

100 percent cotton polos, about $17.
Extra-strong, three-ply, machine-washable cotton sweaters, about $30.
Cotton/polyester chino pants, in khaki only, mailed cuffed or uncuffed to your inseam specifications, about $26.
100 percent cotton oxford cloth shirts, in blue only (now *that's* basic), about $17.

LANDS' END
Lands' End Lane
Dodgeville, WI 53533
800-356-4444

At least two dozen examples of how the mail-order savings strategy can pay off face you from the Lands' End pages. This is where to find basic sweaters at prices you usually have to wait for until the winter or summer clearances. Some sample items:

100 percent wool crew neck Shetland sweaters, about $19.
Crew neck Ragg wool sweaters, about $19. (Almost every outdoor catalogue you pick
up features Ragg wool sweaters. The Ragg wool concept was originally
developed in Iceland. It makes for durable, warm but mid-weight sweaters light enough to wear during outdoor activities. The wool is distin-
guished by its "shaggy" coloring.)
Two-ply British lambswool sweaters, about $26.
A three-button tweed sport coat, featuring real leather buttons, about $120.

SHEPLERS, INC.
6501 West Kellogg
P.O. Box 7702
Wichita, KS 67277
316-943-2151
800-835-4004

This catalogue says, "Howdy, pardner" from first page to last. So much West-ern wear to rope you'll never again have to ride off your ranch to get it. All authentic. All good value. Some sample items:

Sheplers' own cowboys boots start at about $45.
Ornately patterned Western belts with plain and sturdy or rhinestone cowboy buckles start at about $15.
Sheplers' offers the best buys on plain and fancy Western shirts, starting at about $13.
Blue denim Western shirts, at about $17, have a look guaranteed to put you on happy
sartorial trails for a long time. In 100 percent cotton, with pearl snap
buttons on front, pockets and cuffs. Yee-ha.

SOCCER SPORT SUPPLY
1745 First Avenue
New York, NY 10028
212-427-6050
Soccer/rugby gear with a bargain kick. See chapter 10.

SPORTSWEAR CLEARINGHOUSE
Box 173-W4
Winchester, MA 01890
800-227-1617, ext. 761
Discount T-shirts and active sportswear. See chapter 10.

# Fair Trade

The Federal Trade Commission oversees mail-order operations and provides several consumer safeguards making buying by mail more comfortable. One batch of rules deals with the time it takes goods to get from "out there" to your door. Unless a by-mail broker states otherwise in his order blank, he must ship your order within thirty days, or offer you a refund. And requesting a refund shouldn't cost you. The company must offer a cost-free method of informing them (an 800 number, an offer to accept charges on a collect call, etc.). Thus, if a month passes and you: A, don't receive your clothes and, B, don't hear from the company, call its toll-free number or write a letter requesting an explanation.

If after calling or writing you still don't get satisfaction—a rare occurrence when dealing with reputable firms like those listed above—you can seek outside intervention. (The following applies to any complaints you may have concerning a firm's merchandise or service.)

The first agency you should contact is the Direct Mail Marketing Association (DMMA), which operates a Mail-Order Action Line (6 East 43rd Street, New York, NY 10017. 212-689-4977). The DMMA, representing about 70 percent of the country's mail-order businesses, investigates all consumer complaints.

"Most of the complaints we handle deal with mail-order houses not shipping goods ordered," according to Donna Sweeney, a DMMA spokesperson. "But people shouldn't panic if that happens. There are a lot of things that could be stopping you from receiving your merchandise; there are usually extenuating circumstances involved. We resolve 85 percent of the complaints we handle. And that doesn't mean the other 15 percent are disreputable firms; some customers just can't be satisfied."

Send the action line copies of the front and back of any cancelled checks or charge card receipts, tell them the date you ordered, describe the problem and say what you want done about it. The action line will call the firm, getting back to you within two weeks. The DMMA's admirable troubleshooting success record is credited to: muscle within the industry, and a policy of referring unresolved disputes to the Chief Inspector of the U.S. Postal Service (USPS).

You can seek help from the USPS directly, but they're slower to resolve problems. However, if they find the company at fault they can flex their muscles by withholding mail delivery from the firm. Write The Chief Postal Inspector, U.S. Postal Service, Washington, D.C. 20260.

## Cataloguing Catalogues

The following books/pamphlets contain lists of mail-order firms, including those dealing in men's clothing.

"*Direct* Magazine's Catalogue of Mail-Order Catalogues," $3.95 from *Direct* Magazine, 60 East 42nd Street, Suite 1825, New York, NY 10017.

*Directory of Shop-by-Mail Bargain Sources*, by Margaret A. Boyd and Sue Scott-Martin. New York: Pilot Books, 1978.

"The Great Catalogue Guide," $1 from Direct Mail Marketing Association, 6 East 43rd Street, New York, NY 10017.

*Mail Order U.S.A.: A Consumer's Guide to Over 2,000 Top Mail-Order Catalogues in the U.S. and Canada.* Washington, D.C.: Mail-Order Press, 1978.

*The Wholesale-by-Mail Catalogue*, by Lowell Miller. New York: St. Martin's Press, 1979.

# SECONDHAND ROSES

## Used-Clothing
## Savings

A WHOPPING 90 PERCENT OFF.

Imagine securing such savings on your clothing buys. You can, at least sometimes, for many secondhand garments cost only a small fraction of the price of comparable new clothes. Some preworn wearables are quite simply the best garment bargains around. Taking advantage of them, you can slice your clothing bills into easy to swallow, bite-sized bits.

That is, if you only try.

A lot of guys won't. To them, buying used clothing is as off limits as buying used toothbrushes or hair combs. But that's because they've never surveyed the land of retreaded wearables. Until now. Today, more and more men are sidling up to the sweet scent of secondhand roses. Why?

Fifteen or twenty years ago previously worn clothes were about as stylish as used tires. But style has been redefined since the days when dressing right meant wearing the latest styles in specific ways. Today style is an individual matter, not so much what you wear as how you wear it. We take this for granted, but it's nothing less than a revolution making almost all garments, even secondhand varieties, valid vehicles for cruising the style freeway.

Today's loose definition of what's "right" in dressing validates the used-clothing strategy, but another factor popularizing the previously worn is a new sense of value. Today more men are buying the best quality clothes, albeit slightly used, instead of shoddy new threads.

Used-clothing buyers fall into two categories. Some view the savings strategy

*Shoppers frequenting vintage clothing boutiques can put together outfits as fashionable as the latest designer goods, due to the fact that today's best menswear often mimics classic styles from the past.*

as a conveyor belt on which today's styles pass by at drastically reduced rates. Others also shop for vintage menswear originally produced in the 1920s, '30s, '40s and '50s. The latter group of trend-setters usually blend used garments with new, fashionable wearables in a very personalized, eclectic wardrobe mix. And they often race ahead of the fashion pack with some looks. The reason: Designers continually mine styling ideas from past menswear eras, often appearing to copy the clothes worn by those who wear vintage styles. This often occurs when period movies become hits. For example, a few years back the movies *Raiders of the Lost Ark* and *Chariots of Fire* launched a trend in menswear for styles created in the eras in which the movies were set. Vintage-clothing fans hopped on the trend immediately, preceding the designer versions of the same garments by a season.

## Different Drummers

If you care to count, through the years you've probably disposed of enough clothes to fill a small men's boutique. Why did you issue them walking papers? Too worn to wear? Riddled with holes and stains? Completely outdated by new fashion directions? Most likely not. Most likely, like one pizza slice too many, what looked so good before had lost its special attraction. It wasn't the clothes. It was your style evolution. Or maybe you lost weight. Or gained it. Whatever the reason, probably half the threads you disposed of were very wearable, indeed.

OK. Now think of all the guys out there losing weight, gaining weight, remodeling their wardrobes, etc. (not to mention the hordes who get half their wardrobes disposed of by girl friends or wives). Every year millions of men's garments are stitched up and sold. And millions are eased out of closet lineups. Where do these secondhand troops go? You'd be (will be) surprised at the number of rest stops they populate and how easy it is to pick good finds. Five main secondhand sources exist: thrift shops, resale shops, military surplus stores, antique boutiques and flea markets, with other outlets also showcasing secondhand items.

Warehouse volumes of used sartorial supplies are handled by the nation's thrift shops. These enclaves are key source spots for most men employing a secondhand saving strategy. They're run by such national organizations as Goodwill Industries, the Salvation Army and the Junior League, as well as by hundreds of local charities. True thrift shops are nonprofit organizations relying on donations to keep their racks tightly stocked.

Recently entrepreneurs have extrapolated the basic thrift shop idea into profit-making "resale" shops. Springing up as fast as computer stores, they benefit dona-

*Suits from the forties incorporate an esthetically modern bold silhouette.*

tors and buyers alike. The deal: Clothing owners supply items to a resale shop on consignment. The shop prices them and displays them in a boutiquelike setting. When sold, the original owner and the store split profits 50-50.

The entrepreneurial spirit is alive and well at flea markets, too. Holding many small individual collections of wearables, they are yet another source of broken-in wardrobe bargains. Most such setups are open-air markets with sellers displaying their wearable wares on small tables and racks on Saturday and Sunday afternoons.

The varied collections at flea markets make for a potpourri of possible bargain bonanzas. For sheer volume, however, think of this: Lots of guys discard many a decent garment in their lives, but Uncle Sam has sandbagged an army's worth. Several armies' worth, in fact, in the form of military surplus garb funneled through surplus stores. At these depots supplies of sturdy olive, khaki and navy blue soldier and sailor garb have served savvy civilians' needs for decades.

Unlike the armed forces' regimented outfits, some civilian styles develop personalities over the years, which transcend their age with grace and charm. Today such "vintage" clothing is housed in another form of secondhand silo, the antique boutiques. Usually run by fashion-conscious proprietors, these stores offer period menswear of the twenties, thirties, forties and fifties with a smattering of sixties garb. To get a handle on this idea, imagine rummaging through a Salvation Army 50-cent bin in the year 1995 (of course, by then it might be a $5 bin), and finding an Armani linen sport coat. Sure the styling would be antiquated, but would the jacket be less wear worthy?

In addition to the above suppliers, golden oldie menswear can be obtained at such sites as rummage sales, garage sales, estate sales, etc.

That, briefly, is a rundown of secondhand sartorial supply sources—a varied lot with varied stock. More detailed descriptions of the sources just outlined, along with tactical guidelines for shopping them, follow.


## Buried Treasure

Thrift shops are horns of plenty, overflowing with plenty of jewels and plenty of junk. Clothing finds vary from stuff you could never afford to purchase new to deformed rags sporting buttons. The age of thrift shop clothing ranges from months to years, the condition from musty to minty fresh. But one constant remains: Prices are so low they scrape. Suits for $10–$20, pants for $5–$15, shirts from 50 cents to $10. And thrift shops always sport bins of $1 and $2 items worth a search, plus an ever-present half-price sale in one clothing category or another, making them some of the more adventuresome clothes-shopping avenues around.

And they're the friendliest places to shop, usually staffed by good-natured souls donating their time or handicapped individuals ready to help. Maybe it's the something-for-nothing atmosphere, but most thrift shop staffs seem to get as big a kick out of finding you a bargain as you do. And many times you may command preferential treatment, because while menswear is in good supply, menswear customers are not. This is especially true outside big cities, where most men aren't attuned to the charitable deals thrifts dole out. And it's a good feeling knowing the dollars you spend in thrifts are helping more than a clothing producer's balance sheet. If you think only people on bare-bones budgets shop the thrifts, dump the idea and start rifling the retread racks, because today they attract middle- and upper-class citizens. Here are the essential guerrilla tactics to turn a thrift shop survey into an adventuresome outing where pocket change garners prized closet pieces. *Note:* Many of the following shopping strategies apply to all secondhand-clothes shopping.

• First off, to find thrifts just look in the Yellow Pages under Thrift Shops or Charity Organizations. Thrift shops vary in their personalities as much as retail stores. Most have a regular group of contributors, as most people like to associate themselves with specific causes. This means it pays to pinpoint charities in your area that are favorites of the well-to-do. These receive the kind of donations that turn into smart shopping trophies when hung on a $12 rack carrying a half-price sign. Thrifts run by wealthier women's organizations are usually the type of mines yielding such gems.

• In areas of the country where thrift shopping is a popular pastime, much of your success depends on timing. You want to be in the store the day new donations make their entrance. But stores work inventories differently. Some restock the shelves on a specific weekday. Obviously, it pays to get to the store as soon after as possible. Some restock over the weekend. Run early-in-the-week checks on these.

• The prices are so low at thrift shops you wonder why they bother to run sales. But they do. And they're usually of the half-price variety. And when you find a $10 or $20 find at half off, well, that's dressing better for so much less it's, if not magic, then at least a good trick. Some shops have specific sale days. You'll obviously want to attend, so ask when they're scheduled. Other operations run sales pell-mell. For these, ask when their next menswear sale might be.

• Along the same timely lines, some thrifts are the beneficiaries of donated department store samples and overstocks. Divining when such shipments are arriving is the thrift shop equivalent of a hot stock tip.

• When it comes to threading your way through thrift shops there's no better shopping strategy than patient determination. When looking for something specific, however (a brown leather belt, a gray flannel suit in size 42 regular, a red wool scarf) always ask the store staff where it might be. Often what you're looking for is in the shop, but not on display. For example, it could be on a back-room rack. This is almost always true in off-season shopping, as when you're looking for a cotton sweater or bathing suit in December. Also, in smaller shops a "special request" list is sometimes kept. If you're on it, when the brown tweed jacket you've been looking for comes in, you'll be contacted.

▪ If you see something you like and it's cheap (as it will no doubt be), buy it on the spot. You don't have the advantage of mulling over the decision to purchase, because the item is unique and may well vanish before the next setting sun.

Those are some basic thrift shop buying tactics. Now for some shopping tips to help you consistently pull golden garment needles from the haystack of secondhand wear:

▪ Prying stains from older clothes is about as easy as bleaching coal. Unless a spot is ordinary dirt that will vanish in the wash or at the dry cleaners, or unless it's in a hidden area, move along to cleaner clothing pastures.

▪ Try it on. Sizes are often guesstimated by thrift shop staffers. So don't trust tag sizes. Also, suits, sports jackets and pants may have been altered, so you'll want to make sure your bones and bulges match the previous owner's.

▪ Which brings up another point: Always keep the alteration option in mind. If a garment is too big it can be whittled down (however, small sizes can't be enlarged). Also, wide-lapeled jackets and flare-leg pants from the early/late seventies can easily be brought up to date with simple tailoring (see chapter 13). Thus, find beautiful but dated suits in fine wools and wool blends for $15 or $20 at the thrifts, spend $50–$55 to have them updated, and for $70 you've got what might cost $300 off the department store rack. Another such option: making shorts from trousers and short-sleeved shirts from long-sleeved models.

▪ Certain wear and tear signs are bound to show up on secondhand clothes. They still may be good, but knowing when to alter/repair them becomes crucial to your buying decision. As outlined above, alterations can turn stately but outmoded threads into first-class closet citizens. In general, alterations and/or repair work should be considered when you have spotted something special in a high quality fabric (perhaps with a prestigious store label). But the job to make it right shouldn't be too great.

Here's a guide to inspecting the secondhand, and how to decide when to hospitalize wounded sartorial soldiers.

First, the outside. Check for missing buttons. It's a minor repair to replace the whole set (about $10 on a suit), which you'll have to do even if only a single button has jumped ship (except in the case of jacket sleeve buttons, where you can even out the button count by removing the appropriate number from the opposite sleeve). Check zippers. Again, a minor repair (about $7 for pants zippers), but one which might sway your decision to buy. Check for cigarette burns or holes caused by moths, and if you spot them in a noticeable area, forget about fixing them, as the cost of reweaving is too great. On sweaters check for "pilling," when abrasion has caused tiny balls of fiber to form on the fabric's surface. If this isn't too severe (say the pills are few in number and confined to a small area), you can remove them by performing surgery with a razor blade.

Now for the inside. Turn garments inside out and inspect the seams. On sport coats, suit jackets and coats eyeball the armhole and sleeve seams; on trousers the waist-to-crotch seam is most important. Ripped seams are easily resewn (tailoring cost, from $5–$15). But a seam study should also take into account whether there's enough extra fabric (at least ¼" and preferably ½") to allow for alterations.

When you try on garments you'll know if their sleeves or pant legs need lengthening. This is only possible on dark fabrics, and even then a telltale ring from the previous length may show. In general, you can't lengthen sleeves or pant legs on older garb. In addition to seams, the linings of jackets and coats can be a problem. Slightly torn linings are readily and inexpensively resewn ($5–$10). But shredded linings will need complete replacement, which can get costly.

*Note:* When you find the minor damages listed above, use 'em as bargaining leverage. Point out the flaw and ask for a price slash to cover repair costs.


## Navigating the Nearly New

The appeal and availability of high quality, little-worn used clothes has spawned an eighties answer to thrift shops for supplying secondhand wardrobe wares: resale shops. For some men resalers are first-class answers to secondhand clothes. For example, for those short on time they're easier to shop than thrifts; clothes are neatly arranged, clean and readily wearable. And, if you need to ease into the idea of wearing retreaded threads, resalers are good because stores *look* like regular retailers, and clothes *look* new. (And sometimes the clothes are new. Occasionally such shops soak up new merchandise from department stores, acting as outlets.) Some gray clouds dot the resale sky, though, One drawback: Prices are two to three times higher at resalers than at thrifts. Another: Outside large cities resale shops are scarce and the quantity of men's clothing in them small compared to the variety of women's goods or to the menswear available in thrifts. There are exceptions. Some resalers, such as The Closet in Boston, are devoted exclusively to menswear. Resalers do mark down unsold items every few weeks. If something doesn't sell on sale, it may be slash-priced to thrift shop levels.

Shop resalers intelligently by using the tactics outlined for thrifts. Ask about sales, new shipments and specific items, and think in terms of alterations. (Many wide-lapeled suits and jackets and flared pants will be found.)

# Vintage Variety

While resalers display nearly new clothes in boutiquelike settings, antique boutiques stock such storelike spaces with clothes from the 1920s, '30s, '40s, '50s and '60s. Many men who buy such vintage garments are after a unique, fashionable look—sometimes at the expense of savings, as some antique styles cost as much as new clothes. Still, classic and trendy bargains abound at antique boutiques. And few other shopping strategies yield such eye-catching finds.

Perhaps the most attractive aspect of vintage garments is their unique character. Sure, it's true menswear designers continually dip into past style eras, providing us with copies of past menswear products. But the real things are often better made of better fabrics. Many have a kind of patina gained over time. And many, surprisingly, look up-to-the-minute fashionable just because they're different.

Obviously, the idea with these clothes isn't to dress as if you just popped out of a time warp from the forties or fifties. The idea is to mix old with new for a personal look, take the best from the past and mix it with what is going on today. One rule to follow: Stick to clothes you feel comfortable in. Ones needing few, if any, alterations. Now here's a sampling—a smattering, really—of common menswear items you'll find in antique boutiques.

*SHIRTS.* Generally, shirts are the least costly vintage apparel ($5–$15). Some common types: small-collared dress shirts from the sixties, rayon and cotton Hawaiian sport shirts from the fifties, fifties work and sport shirts, wing-collar tuxedo shirts from the forties through the sixties. Many of these styles have served as inspiration for designers in recent years and are that much more wearable for it.

For example, vintage tuxedo shirts started showing up on the streets in the mid-seventies and have been making designer-line appearances ever since. The designer interpretations cost more and lack the crispness of the real things, which you can pick up for under $15.

On a more casual course are fifties Hawaiian shirts. How many times will they come back in style? The vintage variety in rayon or cotton have a loose, easy feeling. Vintage fifties work shirts are brightly colored with a comfortable cut. At $8–$10 they're valid alternatives to many of today's similar styles.

*PANTS.* You'll find lots of dress pants from the fifties. Most will be pleated, with tapered legs. Some common forties finds are pleated, cuffed pants in baggy silhouettes. Also available: black forties and fifties tuxedo pants with satin side stripes, and plain front, straight-leg khakis from the fifties and sixties. Probably your best bet (aside from a spare pair of khakis) are dark, pleated, slightly tapered fifties dress pants. (The baggier versions don't have the right proportions for today's jackets.) Vintage pants cost $10–$25. For such a small investment in the past, you can always consider altering a pair into walking shorts.

*Secondhand tuxedoes are plentiful and stylish.*

SUITS/SPORT JACKETS. Finding well-worth-buying suits and sport jackets on the oldie goldie racks can be a long search in big city antique boutiques. And while their prices are as vintage as their styling ($25–$40 for suits, $15–$30 for sport jackets), most are fifties and sixties generated, with narrow lapels and somber colors. When narrow lapels were fashionable, these were great buys and no doubt will be again when lapel widths swing to the skinny side of the proportion pendulum. Now they look odd. Double-breasted forties models are better bets. Broad shouldered, broad lapeled, with fitted waists, they carry a European swagger (even though Europe borrowed this silhouette from America). Other best bets: forties and fifties unconstructed jackets. While today's manufacturers have idled the unconstructed idea, the older models look and feel as good as ever.

COATS. Winter wool coats are, simply, the best antique boutique buys. Why? A modern winter wool warmer, even when poached from a cold-weather clearance sale, costs at least $125. At antique boutiques, old chesterfields and raglan-sleeved, full-length overcoats of better quality are had for $40–$70 (half that in summer). As older, heavier wool coating material wears only slightly less hardily than iron mail, many coats are in brand-new shape. Several vintage wool overcoat selections should be scouted before purchasing a new winter number.

## In the Trenches

A dress-for-less strategy winning budget battles since WWII, military surplus garb can easily aid your fight for a less expensive wardrobe. Surplus garb delivers solid support forces in a number of ways. For one thing, military inspired styling is continually cropping up in designer menswear collections. This makes sense, as over the centuries military uniforms have contributed many specific styling features to civilian wear. Thus, military styling is familiar. Then there is the simplicity, quality and functionalism of soldier wear. Most is made of all cotton or wool and constructed to withstand rigorous wear (sturdy sewing, weighty zippers, tough buttons, etc.).

At the typical army surplus store you'll find uniforms from the battle forces of the world. New or secondhand, their prices depend on the action they've seen. Some styles to look for: field jackets, trench coats, fatigue pants, pea coats and bomber jackets. Find surplus stores in the Yellow Pages under Clothing-Surplus or Surplus Merchandise.

## Market Values

No other used-clothing forum demonstrates previously worn clothing's popularity as well as flea markets. The fleas are everywhere today, and used clothing is their main attraction. They're usually held on weekends in large parking lots or warehouse-type buildings. Miscellaneous sellers bring their clothes and household objects to be sold, setting them up on tables and racks to create sprawling one-day markets. To find the fleas in your area, check out the classified ads in weekly newspapers under Miscellaneous Sales.

Strolling among a flea market's scattered tables can make for a pleasant and sartorially profitable Saturday or Sunday afternoon. Variety is the byword. You never know when you'll come across the kind of flea finds that keep you itching for more.

Most flea market vendors are total amateurs when it comes to selling. Prices are arbitrary, varying with the time of day, amount of customers, what a vendor ate for breakfast, etc. Since prices usually aren't set in stone or, for that matter, even written on a tag, hardball bargaining occurs on just about everything.

Actually, bargaining is a savings tactic you can apply to most secondhand

All-wool overcoats from the thirties, forties and fifties are some of the best used clothing buys.

Military surplus gear isn't all khaki and olive drab. Items like this white canvas French naval officer's uniform, sporting gold buttons and a comfortable cut, can easily be brought into active duty.

Military shirts and pants can help win your clothing budget battles.

clothes. The dealers at thrifts, resale shops, antique boutiques and surplus stores are all used to it. You should be too. It can save you 10 to 20 percent on most of your secondhand roses. Here are some secondhand clothes bargaining tips applying to flea markets and all the sources outlined in the chapter.

Perhaps the best reason for a price reduction from your standpoint is a flaw in the garment. It doesn't have to be big or even very noticeable. It can be normal wear. You can still point to it and ask for a price reduction, since the clothing is worn/damaged. Sometimes you can raise the point that a competitor's table (at fleas) or store has a similar garment for a lot less money. Ask the person you're bargaining with if they'll meet the competitor's price. (Whether there really has to be such a competitor is up to you.) If you're planning to buy more than one garment, you have loads of bargaining leverage. You might ask if two garments can be bought for the price of one. Or ask for a substantial cut in the total cost of a group of items. In general, a relaxed, aw-come-on, we're-all-friends-here approach works best when bargaining at flea markets. When dealing with pros, a harder sharper edge may be needed to initiate a price cut.

*Note:* Some flea markets are value oases for new, designer merchandise, too. Every Sunday, millions of dollars' worth of name-brand clothes by Sassoon, Sergio Valente, Arrow, Robert Bruce, Levi Strauss, LaCoste, etc., spend their weekends on flea market tables, where they sell for well below retail levies. Such goods usually get to the fleas by devious routes. Perhaps a vendor has an "uncle" in the clothing business who, as a favor, lets him sell small quantities of merchandise. Maybe the goods are stolen. Or maybe, as a result of flea market popularity, a retailer buys more stock from a manufacturer than he needs, then sells the extra amount on Sundays for just over wholesale. Whatever, there are deals to be had.

There are also rip-offs. This is because fleas are big outlets for counterfeit designer goods. For example, at a recent flea market outing polo shirts labeled "Polo by Ralph Lauren" were being sold for $10 apiece. The shirts were 60 percent polyester/40 percent cotton (all the designer's polos are 100 percent cotton) and the Polo logo was so badly sewn as to be unrecognizable.

# House Cleanings

Thrift and resale shops, antique boutiques, military surplus stores and flea markets are only some of the gardens growing secondhand roses. There are others. Here's a quick rundown:

*ESTATE SALES.* Very good sources for vintage clothing and high quality contemporary wearables and accessories. These sales are listed in newspaper classifieds. Since most of the action at them centers on furniture and appliances, you may be able to deal on a group of garments.

*RUMMAGE SALES.* The precursors to flea markets, rummage sales can offer better quality than the fleas at a lower price. The sales are held by churches and charitable organizations, who may place ads in small newspapers or post the dates and times on community bulletin boards. A big rummage sale can be a great find, for lots of men's clothing will have been donated, but women, mostly, will attend.

*GARAGE/APARTMENT SALES.* Perhaps the cheapest source for secondhand clothes. Many times shirts and pants will carry 25 or 50 cent prices. With luck, you'll be able to nickel and dime yourself into some great buys. The drawback: There's usually not much of a selection. One solution: Check the newspaper classifieds for garage sales, finding three or four in roughly the same area, and hit them all in a single morning.

*POST OFFICE AUCTIONS.* An interesting alternative to seeking secondhand finds at flea markets or home sales. Post office auctions are held at the post office's nineteen dead-parcel branches approximately eight times a year. What will you find? You never know until you go. At the auctions a jumbled assortment of items are placed in boxes. These are numbered. You're allowed to poke through the boxes one hour before auction time. When it rolls around, you bid on the boxes you want. The post office's dead-parcel offices are located in Atlanta; Bell, California; Boston; Chicago; Cincinnati; Denver; Detroit; Fort Worth; Greensboro; Jacksonville; Memphis; New York; Philadelphia; Pittsburgh; St. Louis; St. Paul; San Francisco; Seattle; and Washington, D.C.

*DRY CLEANERS.* You'd be surprised at the number of unclaimed clothes dry cleaners get stuck with. Ask your cleaner if he has any you might be interested in. He should sell them to you very inexpensively.

That's the secondhand story. Budget pinched or budget balanced, it's a strategy affording huge savings on often spectacular sartorial fare.

## ▪ 6 ▪

# MAN POWER

## How Clothing Salesmen
## Can Save You Money

SOME clothing salesmen would sell you their store's dressing rooms if you would buy. That's why most men trust menswear salesmen about as much as they do growling Doberman pinschers. ("They're just after a commission," "They know as much about what I like as I know about selling clothes," etc.) Some misgivings are justified. Historically, clothing salesmen haven't been known to have your best interests at heart.

But that's only the dark side of the salesman story.

The bright side: The right salesperson can *save* you money on clothing. That's right, save. A good salesman is a sartorial financial advisor—recommending winning investments, steering you clear of dismal dividend payers.

But what separates the good from the bad? The hucksters from the heaven sent? Before learning how dirty players deal, how superb sales help saves, how to pick the conscientious from the cons, it would be helpful to see, from a salesman's perspective, the interaction between shopper and clothes seller. You know how *you* approach buying clothes. How do salesmen—good *and* bad—approach selling them?

## Overtures

When you enter a men's shop or men's department you're sized up faster than a bikini on the beach. Not for the same reasons, of course. But before you've said a word the salesmen are pegging you.

Since they pick up, put down, hold, fold and bag clothing about as often as you inhale, and since they often have time to think about the language of clothing, they make most of their inferences from how you're dressed. Do you have money to spend? Are you a tough customer or a friendly type? Are you just killing time? Are you interested in the latest fashions or basic styles? How you're dressed says it all to salesmen.

If you walk in and don't make any sort of overture to the store staff—say you just start browsing—then a salesman will approach and ask if he can help you. All salesmen do this. It's their job. And both good and bad will begin by trying to break the inherent barrier between you by trying to dispel all those thoughts in your head telling you, "This guy is out to break my bank." This disarmament attempt usually takes the form of a polite smile, but some salesmen give their names and offer a handshake.

Now, more than half the Joes a salesman asks to help say, "Just looking." Some mumble it into a rack of raincoats or pants without ever looking to see who's asking. Some smile when they say it. Whatever, this is frustrating to salesmen ("Why doesn't anyone ever say, 'Gosh, I was hoping you'd ask!'?"). But it goes with the selling space, so to speak. So while you just browse you're analyzed some more. What do you look at? What do you touch? What sizes do you check out? Salesmen note all this, quickly compiling a file on what types of clothes interest you.

After a few more ticks of the clock the salesman will again approach and ask if he might help you. If you decline, he might decide to wait until *you* ask *him*. Or he might, implementing his observations, comment on some clothes in the area. ("Those sweaters look great under sport jackets.")

This type of discreet interaction continues until you bring a garment to the cash register, or give some sign that you're going to let the salesman play a part in your clothing purchase. It's then, when given the go-ahead to help, that he either starts promoting your best interests or his own ego and/or commission.

There are basic clothes-selling rules by which both good and bad garment hawkers play. For example, if you're shopping with a woman, salesmen assume she's "the decision maker." Why? Because three-quarters of the time she is. No matter how far men travel toward acquiring an interest in clothing, for most the journey doesn't mean beans if their women don't agree with their selections. If *she* likes it, it's great. Another commonality: All salesmen try to come across as veritable rock-hewn pyramids of self-assuredness to instill you with confidence in their ability. And all clothes sellers like to describe the benefits of the clothes under discussion in terms applying to you. ("You say you like blue? Well, *these* shirts are in a blue that would complement your coloring.") Of course, good and bad salesmen employ entirely different approaches within the above rules.

And it's the approach you must judge. Because there are two ways you can save money with salesmen. One is to avoid the bad ones. The second is to let good salesmen do their best work for you.

## Misguided Opinions

First let's get to know the less-than-model salesman. If you can recognize him, you can distance yourself from less-than-satisfying shopping experiences. I happen to know such a clothes seller. He works in a men's shop close to my home. Let's call him Dave.

Dave embodies most of the negative traits associated with his profession. But he doesn't look or act the part. For example, he's short and soft spoken. Yet, poised with suit in hand, he commands attention as if wielding a deadly weapon. His powers of persuasion, which he applies rather ruthlessly, never cease to amaze, and to some onlookers might even appear amusing. For example, I once saw him sell a suit to a man who, at the very least, wore a size 38 regular. Dave sold him a 36 short, the jacket's cuffs resting closer to this man's elbows than his wrists. ("The tailor will just let them all the way down. *It's simple!*" explained Dave.)

Why does he do it? Ask him while in the store and he dismisses the question with, "The commission." But there's obviously something more. How does he do it? *That's* important. Because you want to be able to recognize the Daves, scattered like bear traps in men's shops across the country, and avoid them. To find out the whys and hows behind Dave's selling I asked if we might meet over lunch, so that he could lend some insight into how he sells, and why unwary customers buy. He agreed. In his own sobering words, this is what he said.

"I love selling. And the whole secret to selling is revving yourself up. It's all in your mind. Selling is people believing in you, because most people who come to buy things don't know anything. When they come in, they're actually looking for your advice.

"Never be in doubt, because once you're in doubt the customer is in doubt of you, and you'll never sell to him.

"I always remain in control. Customers will try to say, 'I know this and I know that and I know what fits me right.' Never let a customer do that. He has to believe that *you* know what looks good on him, because deep down inside that's what they're looking for—your opinion.

"The best way to approach a person is to start up a conversation, because it gets his mind off spending money. They hate to spend money. So I get into another topic. The best one, I find, is to go up to the person and, even if they look bad, tell them they look great. They think, 'Hey, this guy knows what he's talking about.' That's the first thing I do. Then I would most likely tell him how the garment he tries on looks and how it fits, how it should look, and how it should fit on him. You see, once I start talking they stop talking, and that's what you have to do, have them stop talking, because if they stop talking they start listening, and then they start believing.

"If you really want to sell a guy, you don't give him one second to have one word. You just jump on him, because if you give him time to think he'll say, 'I'll come back.' Never let a guy tell you that.

"When a guy comes in with a girl friend or wife you don't sell to the guy, you sell to her, because 99 percent of the guys, when they're with their girls, don't care what you tell them. They care what their girl friend or wife tells them, and even if they like something, they won't buy if she doesn't like it. So you sell to her, and if you sell her, you sell him.

"Guys who ask, 'You think this fits right?' I tell, '*Of course* it fits right!'

"Whether I try to sell something that doesn't fit well totally depends on the person. If the person gets me in the wrong mood, yeah, I'll admit I've sold some things that weren't worth a penny. But I said to myself, 'This person is going to buy. They're going to walk out of the store with it.' To me, they must have it, and I make them believe they must have it, that it's something they need, that it's a necessity, which in reality it's not.

"Some of the other salesmen say I treat people like garbage. I do, but only the ones that think they know something.

"Very rarely do I let a customer walk out with just what they came in for. What I say is, 'You know what would go *so* good with that jacket, what would really complement it?' Then I show him a shirt. Then I stop the conversation and go to another topic while he's walking to the dressing room. When he comes out I say, 'Oh, it looks fantastic on you! No! But this tie I have would look beautiful on you. I have to show you this tie!' And I work it from there.

"How much I sell depends on the mood I'm in, no matter who the customers are."

# A Sucker Every Minute

Selling you clothes is a thought encamped in every salesman's cerebral cortex. That's his job. But salesmen like Dave see selling as a singular goal. To them you're a walking wallet waiting to be emptied. You obviously must eliminate these guys from the clothes-buying experience. To help you, here's a list of common ploys crummy salesmen often practice.

*FAST TALK.* You can tell a salesman who revels in "the pitch." He doesn't explain. He jabbers as if auctioning cattle. ("HeyfriendhaveIgotanumberforyou- justtakeyourcoatoffandslipthis . . .") Such a charlatan will give the distinct impression that he cares as much about you as he does about ants under his footsteps. Give him the same consideration.

*POWER PLAYS.* All salesmen seek control of the selling situation, in part because this increases your confidence in them. But such control shouldn't turn to bullying. For example, you might say you never wear green. But your friend insists you try a green sport coat on because it's the "in" color. In reality it may be the only

*Sage salesmen fit you to clothing,
not clothing to you.*

*Four ploys used by salesmen are, clockwise from top left,
fast talk, insincere flattery, pushiness and exaggerated clothing claims.*

color in your size. If you express opinions and your salesman disregards them out of hand, he's a lemon.

"SWITCHEROOS." If you're looking for something specific and the store doesn't have it, the slimy salesman will try to sell you anything else, even if the item is totally dissimilar. To force you into taking his apple instead of your orange, he may discount your original choice, saying something like, "Why would you want that? Nobody wears those anymore. Now this . . .")

IMPOSSIBLE DREAMS. Watch out for hucksters dispensing exaggerated clothing claims such as, "That suit makes you look 50 pounds lighter," "You can wear this shirt anywhere" or "This jacket would cost you five times as much anywhere else." Such attempts to impart magical qualities to clothes are signs of a snake-oil salesman.

ONLY THE BEST WILL DO. "Trading up" describes an attempt at getting you to buy more expensive clothes than you're accustomed to. Better salesmen do this by pointing out the differences in quality and design between lower and higher priced garments. They also respect your wishes if you set a price limit for what you're interested in.

Not the slippery salesman. For example, you'll tell the man you're ready to spend up to $150 on a sport coat. He slips a $300 number on your back and starts rattling off its overwhelming qualities, trying his damnedest to make you feel like a shmuck for thinking of anything less expensive.

*FLATTERY WILL GET HIM EVERYWHERE.* Statements like, "I've never seen a pair of pants fit so well" or "You look like a million bucks in that" are so transparent. But such cheap psychology is the most effective selling ploy insincere salesmen throw you. Everyone likes to think the clothes they buy make them look great. But good salesmen confine their comments to reality.

*YES-MEN.* It's nice to be able to count on your salesman's opinion. But one selling tactic often used by bad salesmen is to agree with everything you say. (You: "This fits pretty good." Him: "Perfect." You: "And this lemon/lime color makes me seem slimmer." Him: "It really does.") This selling strategy is perhaps more pleas-

*Good salesmen take into account your needs, wants and opinions, but can offer sound advice based on their expertise.*

ant than bullying tactics, but just as insincere. You want someone who'll take into account your needs, wants and opinions. But also someone who can offer sound advice based on his expertise.

*VANISHING ACT.* You've tried it on, you've checked it in the mirror, but you can't make up your mind whether to buy. Do you need it? Do you really want it? Will it fit in the wardrobe? Does it offer value? Will the girl friend or wife like it? Logically you know that, unless it's on sale, the chances of it being sold within twenty-four hours are about as good as you finding the money to buy it under your pillow. But you don't want to blow it. Well, salesmen who'll do anything not to blow a sale will say something like, "Better buy it now. They're selling so fast it'll be gone by sunset."

## Saving Graces

Fortunately, most salesmen aren't out to skin you of every cent. Most know the tricks and have used them. But they're wise to this, too: They can only burn you once. Doing so nixes the chance for fetching future dimes from your pockets.

Good salesmen are everywhere. Men's specialty shops, in particular, make a point of hiring professionals and often provide extra customer services to back them up. And big department stores make some effort to train sales staffs. But conscientious salesmen can be discovered lighting the prudent-purchasing path at discounters, too.

## Enlightened Interest

The difference between mediocre or downright bad salesmen and good ones is the difference between *selling* and *servicing*. You want a consultant, not a pitch artist. A pro knowing menswear from sole to collar, one as ready to give counsel as take money. To help you find such gents, here are some traits characterizing quality sales help.

*ICEBREAKER.* As mentioned, salesmen try to break the barrier you invariably erect between yourself and sales help. After introducing himself, a good salesman will put you at ease with his professional approach. Part of this is asking questions pertinent to your purchase.

For example, he will want to know what you do for a living, what type of people you deal with in your business, what, if any, problems you've had with fit in the past and what brands of clothing you like/dislike. He will *act* like a consultant, so the next time you come to the store (hopefully because you were so pleased with your previous purchases), you'll want to seek him out.

*READY AND WILLING.* One of the most pleasant traits a salesman can possess is patience. That means answering your questions fully, explaining how various clothing concepts affect you, making sure you know why you're buying, and that you're comfortable with the decision.

*SECOND CHANCE.* If you're looking for something specific and the store doesn't have it, the good salesman will suggest alternatives (a well-mannered switcheroo). But if they won't do, he will try to order your original request for you, offer to call you when the store gets in something similar to what you want, or tell you of another store where you can find it.

*LATER-DAY SAINT.* If you need time to ponder a clothes-acquisition decision, you don't want to hear, "You'll be sorry . . ." Someone who's *servicing* rather than selling will offer to hold the garment in question for twenty-four hours and may even call you before putting it back on the floor.

*JUSTIFIABLY SO.* It's tough for you to know why, in the same store, similar garments carry wildly dissimilar price tags. Is it the fabric? Construction? Design? The—let's hope not—European-sounding label? But if you can't tell why a garment is more expensive, why should you spend the extra money?

Good salesmen can tell you what makes a $350 suit $100 better than one priced at $250. Getting specific about fabric content, workmanship and detailing, country of origin, and a maker's or designer's reputation.

*FITTING AND PROPER.* Sage salesmen fit you to clothing, not clothing to you. This is basic service, but many salesmen can't or won't provide it. It's based on the fact that each manufacturer embues clothes with a unique cut.

The classic illustration is a broad-shouldered, large-chested American man who tries to fit into a European suit cut as slim as a breadstick. If he doesn't know better, and the salesman doesn't tell him, he will go the next larger size. Result: an awkward-looking square peg of a man in a round hole of a suit.

Between a "European" and an "American" cut, there's a wide spectrum composed of an inch here and a curve there. The right salesman can match your inches and curves to a suit's. And if he doesn't have the suit to do it, he'll tell you so.

*TWO FOR THE MONEY.* Salesmen handle more suits, shirts and ties in a day than you do in a month. Good salesmen put this expertise to use by giving you the most for your money. Here's how. Say you buy a blue blazer. Your salesman should be able to match up shirts and ties giving the blazer two looks, one casual, the other elegant.

*RECORD TIME.* Better salesmen (usually in better stores) keep you on paper. At least that part of you pertinent to wardrobe purchases. Information on the suits in your wardrobe, what brands you prefer, your coloring, whether you travel for business, etc. Thus, when you drop by, the salesman has a ready reference guide to help him guide you.

*DIAL TONES.* Service-oriented salesmen often request your phone number. It isn't so they can call to bum a loan if business is slack, it's to serve you better. For example, they might call several weeks after selling you a suit to see how it's performing. Another example: If you happen to like a certain suit line, your salesman will call to tell you when the new season's shipment has arrived. Or he might arrange a preseason preview. How? When a new season's stock is in the store, but the season is weeks away, the salesman sets aside a dozen new suits in your size, making an appointment with you to inspect them.

## Team Spirit

So you're after salesmen who will service as well as sell, conscientious consultants helping to trim the risks of harvesting lemons from menswear's golden groves. What do you do when you find them?

Turn them into the partners they want to be. Face it: It's difficult, no matter how burnished your style sense, to walk off the street into a wealth of clothing possibilities and pick the perfect item. If nothing else, it takes time to look at what's offered; instead of just browsing you could be sizing up specific selections. Good salesmen can offer these, will help you build a better, more functional (a.k.a. money-pinching) wardrobe and save you from wasting money on misguided purchases.

Maximizing a good salesman's services takes some effort. But before exploring the mechanics of such a partnership, here are some tips on getting the most from *any* salesman you deal with.

*BIG SPENDER.* Act like you're going to buy even if you're not. Salesmen will jump through hoops to please a buyer; roll over and play dead for "just lookers."

*KIND SIR.* Be human. Some men, thinking all salesmen are out to beat the bucks from their wallets, act like they're talking with some sort of contagious subspecies. Acting civilized automatically wins you points.

*DRESS TO THRILL.* You've probably heard this, and it's true: Since salesmen base so many decisions about you on the way you're dressed, it pays to look sharp when shopping. You look like you're serious about clothing—and buying.

*BOSS MAN.* If shopping with a woman, make it clear you're the decision maker. The best way to accomplish this is, when a salesman offers his help, take a step forward and answer for yourself. That's all it takes.

*MULTIPLE CHOICE.* If your salesman is matching shirts and ties to wear with a sport jacket or suit, ask him to put together several suitable combinations, then pick the ones you like best.

*LEMON AID.* Save yourself time, energy and money by detaching yourself from a lemon salesman as soon after you spot him as possible. Tell him, firmly, that you don't need his help.

*REPEAT PERFORMANCE.* Be a return customer. *Nothing* nets you better help faster than a previous purchase.

Once you establish a relationship with a good salesman, working with him is as relaxed an experience as slipping into a trusted barber's chair. This is what you're working toward. How can you help bring about this happy state of affairs? Once you've found a fellow you can trust, here's how to help him serve you better.

*PROPER SCHOOLING.* Let the salesman educate you. For example, when he shows you a new style, ask how it differs from the previous season's. Find out why some suit cuts look better on you, what colors are best for you, how to coordinate your purchases with other items in your wardrobe. It doesn't cost anything to listen, and you can always let your personal tastes dictate whether to buy or not.

*BIG MOUTH.* You have some teaching to do yourself. Tell your clothes counselor your preferences for colors, fabrics, patterns, stripes, fit, the favorite suits in your wardrobe, the ones you wish you hadn't bought, as well as your business duties, etc.

Once you develop partnerships with good salesmen in your favorite stores, shopping will become a more enjoyable, and less expensive, pastime. A last example of this: Once your salesman becomes a partner, he should volunteer information on the store's sales, special purchases, etc.

After all, your being a friend in need should make your salesman a friend indeed.

# 7

# WRONG BUT NOT FORGOTTEN

## Saving with
## Imperfect Apparel Bargains

LIKE a starlet's beauty mark, a small flaw on a prime piece of menswear can be enticing. Not for the same reasons, of course. The pleasing consequence of a garment's imperfection is the glamorous price break it creates. And what could be a prettier sight to budget-conscious eyes?

Loads of slightly tarnished, reduced-price wearables are out there ready to bring a savings shine to your wardrobe. True, flaws must be minor enough so as not to produce aesthetic drag, or be easily fixable, but such garments are readily had.

## Foregone Conclusion

"Irregulars" (imperfect garments) and damaged clothes are a natural by-product of manufacturing and selling menswear.

"Manufacturers make plenty of boo-boos," commented one garment maker. "There isn't a manufacturer, no matter what quality of clothes he's producing, that doesn't have irregulars on every cutting he makes." ("Cutting" is an integral step in clothing production.) Why isn't there a 100 percent success rate for delivering perfect clothing to prospective stores? Why can't it be punched out like so many printed circuits?

That's just it. Manufacturing menswear isn't a nuts and bolts hard-goods industry. Rather, the various fabrics and materials going into wearable products are about as uniform as the colors on alley cats, making the production of menswear an inexact endeavor. Result: imperfections *and* smart-shopper savings. As for damages, there are plenty of those, too, caused by a myriad of circumstances.

# Cause and Effect

From the Federal Trade Commission's (F.T.C.) standpoint, there's a difference between irregulars and seconds. Irregulars (i.r.'s in clothing-industry lingo) sport minor goofs—such fluffs as a puckered spot on silk, an oil stain from a sewing machine, or botched stitching that's shaggy, but still strong. Seconds are less solidly built. They have a rip, tear, cut or pull—something that might affect a garment's actual wearing power.

In practice the F.T.C.'s definitions matter as much as if they'd declared which kind of cheese the moon is made of. Everybody in the garment business speaks of i.r.'s, period. And manufacturers tell their own inspectors what does and doesn't constitute an i.r. These "quality codes" are as uniform as snowflakes. Strict, moderate and oh-what-the-hell-let-it-go codes are equally common.

Some manufacturers equip inspectors with rulers, which they use to verify stitches per inch. Thus, if eighteen stitches per inch is the standard and a shirt comes off the line tacked together with only fourteen per inch—bingo, an irregular. (You would never notice such an inconsistency—that's the lure of near-perfect manufacturer's mistakes.) Other makers don't mind if their shirts incorporate fourteen or four stitches to the inch, so long as they're not, excuse the expression, coming apart at the seams.

Still, most irregulars skirt the norm in more important respects than stitches per inch. Usually i.r.'s are imperfect in their color, weave, knit, size, fit or finish. The trouble comes at one of three phases of clothing manufacture: at the fabric mill, where cloth is initially woven or knitted; the pattern cutter's, where this cloth is cut into puzzlelike pieces; or the sewing factory, where these puzzlelike pieces are stitched together into clothing.

If a cloth mill weaves or knits a botched run of fabric, you can be sure irregular time is right down the line. For example, the mill whips up a fine striped suit fabric. The stripes are ½" apart. Except in a 50 yard section, where ⅝" stripes prevail. When suits are cut and sewn from these wrong-woven goods, the minor spacial incongruity appears in, say, twenty suits.

Or the mill dyes red T-shirt fabric in slightly different shades. Result: Shirts are sewn up with crimson backs and near-crimson fronts. Pattern cutters, who take raw fabric, lay it out, and cut it into pattern pieces to be sewn, are supposed to inspect fabric for faults, but can miss mistakes in weaves and dyes.

And speaking of fabric cutters, "A million things can go wrong" at the pattern-cutting factory, according to the manager of one such facility. Some examples: When cutters lay fabrics out, they pile them piece atop piece, as many as 400 pieces high. In the process, they stretch them taut and secure them in place. A garment's pattern is then laid atop this pile of fabric and cut around with a pattern saw.

Now if the fabric is stretched too taut, when the pattern saw hits it, the cloth "jumps in" a ½" or 1" to the cloth's natural dimensions. Result: too-small pattern pieces, and when the pieces are sewn, too-small garments. But perhaps such a small-sized garment would fit you just right. Again, such "perfect" irregulars make saving with this strategy aesthetically painless.

Other possible pattern problems: The fabric shifts while being cut; or the pattern cutter gets reckless and saws off a corner here or an inch there. Result: 200–400 irregulars. A final example of cutting blunders: Today many large fabric-cutting plants are computerized. But, as one manufacturer pointed out, "The computers are only as good as their operators." A wrong instruction to the electronic brain—say, programming the computer-controlled cutter to make a jacket sleeve an inch too short—and more irregulars leave the factory to populate bargain landscapes.

The sewing factory provides a playground of opportunities to muff menswear production, too. Usually mistakes occur in "topstitching"—stitches meant to be seen, such as the orange thread on blue jeans. These errors are readily noticeable, but many in-the-seam slipups are virtually invisible. Not to irregular catchers, though. They'll spot them coming off the line and demote the garment to i.r. status. Other sewing slipups: belt loops spaced unevenly, misplaced pockets, "bumpy" armhole seams, etc.

But again, irregulars aren't always that irregular. Many quality-garment makers view any slipups along the path from fabric mill to factory delivery as adequate reason for an i.r. marking. "If there's any defect in the stitching whatsoever, we consider it an i.r.," said a spokesman for Levi Strauss jeans.

A spokesman for Bass, the company famous for its businesslike loafers, explained that shoe production offered a number of opportunities for manufacturing errors. "One thing about quality shoe manufacturing is that much of the work is still done by hand," according to the spokesman. "While some processes are automated, hand sewing leaves room for variation. And when those variations are outside the realm of acceptability, you've got an irregular." And savings. Bass sells its irregulars through a chain of outlets at 35 to 40 percent below regular retail prices.

## Heat Treats/Wet Bets

A farmer can harvest a crop of corn as golden as the sun itself. That's still no assurance it will roll into your supermarket with a fresh face. Or keep a golden countenance once there. Menswear is like that. A lot can happen to blemish its pretty face between factory finish and ring-out at the retail register. And when damages do take root, the harvest of savings is sweet indeed.

*While fire and smoke can cause irreparable damage to clothes, oftentimes garments will emerge from such calamities unscathed.*

The main damage-causing agents are fire and water, although many unforeseen events might cause clothes to become less than perfect, forcing a markdown. How can such catastrophes occur? A sprinkler pipe is hit by a forklift and a storage room is flooded. Or a water pipe freezes in winter, bursting and causing a flood. Or a fire breaks out in a men's shop, soaking hundreds of garments in thick smoke, etc., etc.

Most stores incurring fire or water damage on menswear *don't*, as popularly believed, hold "fire" or "water" sales. This is because they can't sell the goods new, and it's bad for their image to sell it used. In addition, damaged merchandise usually has to be removed in order for the store to clean up and resume normal business operations. This last point is important, because in order to clean up, usually *all* merchandise must be removed from the store. This includes un-*damaged* as well as damaged goods.

Rather than hold a special sale, when a menswear retailer is hit by fire or flood, his insurance company steps in, appointing one or more "salvors" to rid the store of merchandise, so a cleanup can begin. Salvors restore such clothes to good condition, then sell them to retailers specializing in "distressed" (damaged) merchandise or, if the clothes weren't damaged at all, menswear discounters.

"Damages occur on a regular basis, about once a week for menswear," said a branch manager of the M. F. Bank salvor operation, which operates twenty offices across the U.S., as well as a 200,000-square-foot distressed-merchandise store in Minneapolis. "Last week we took over 4,000 men's Sassoon suits, due to a rack collapse. The suits had been hanging in storage, and when the rack fell to the floor some of the suits were pinched or had their fabric torn. They were soiled considerably, because a lot of the ceiling and walls came down with the rack. We sent them to our Minneapolis store, which has a dry cleaning operation to clean soiled clothing."

Of course, singed or soaked stores may hold their own sales, selling clothes "as is." In such cases it's up to you to decide whether it's worth trying to clean them or not. (More on this later.)

## Wounded in Action

"Shopworn" clothes populate *every* men's shop and men's clothing department *every* season. These are the once-healthy garments that, somewhere along the line, suffered an accident. They're the returned clothes brought back in bad shape; or the clothes smudged by careless shoppers, or soiled from a salesman's clutsy handling; the shirts missing buttons, the raincoats missing belts; the sweaters sporting threads hanging like vines on walls.

Some stores prefer donating such clothes to charity rather than admitting they exist. But most set aside a rack or two for shopworn goods at the end of a season, also including in such selections irregulars discovered by shoppers when goods such as shirts and sweaters were removed from their packaging.

Such in-store damaged goods are sold as is, with prices as low as damages are serious. Sometimes flaws are labeled, describing defects so you know what "as is" is, so to speak. In other instances one must play Scotland Yard in inspecting such items. Unfortunately, divining when stores will put out a rack of shopworn items is impossible. After all, it's no cause for the store to celebrate—or advertise. They usually appear at season's end. But you can always ask a salesperson when a store's damaged sale will commence.

## Disabled Glory

There are several rules governing the irregular and damaged-goods game, and several strategies you can employ to wring savings-graced wearables from it.

First, the F.T.C. says irregulars and seconds should be branded as such. It's an "unfair deceptive practice in commerce" *not* to label i.r.'s and so-called seconds.

The most general rule regarding prices is that they usually indicate the distance from perfection at which imperfect garments orbit. Thus, the most profitable irregular/damaged shopping boils down to this: Find merchandise from a quality manufacturer to begin with, and find it in near-perfect condition.

A few irregulars you discover will be, abnormally, perfect. Others will have suffered a disabling casualty, precluding them from joining your wardrobe's ranks. Most will carry no-show flaws, or a blemish easily and inexpensively repaired. Below are some specific hunting hints for bagging irregular and damaged closet trophies.

*Look for irregular or damaged clothing you can wear as is.*
*If you'll be wearing a jacket and tie, and really scrimping,*
*only a shirt's cuffs and collar need be perfect.*

▪ Irregular and distressed merchandise is the mainstay of discounters, odd-lot merchants and damaged-goods specialists. Discounters only handle irregulars and practically perfect damages (their main stock being off-price merchandise; see chapter 1 for a nationwide listing). Hundreds of distressed-merchandise merchandisers are scattered across the country. To find them, look in the Yellow Pages under Men's Apparel or Retail Stores—Damaged Goods.

▪ Look for clothes you can wear as is. For example, a shirt with a hole in the chest area can't be worn off the rack. One with the same sized hole in back, or low enough so that it can't be seen when the shirt's tucked in, might be. And if you'll be wearing the shirt with a jacket, only the collar, cuffs, and chest/stomach areas need be perfect.

▪ Clothes marred by surface dirt need only be washed or dry cleaned. Stains are another matter. If in a noticeable area, your purchase is, frankly, a dice roll. You may be inclined to chance it, however, if the price doesn't threaten to break your bank.

▪ Better stores offer better irregulars at season's end because of a quality consciousness that may exceed your own. Charging the prices they do, ritzy retailers can't afford to sell garments even slightly marred. So check such stores' policies, readying yourself for the day they discreetly display expensive-if-perfect imperfects.

▪ You may be able to play the ol' "end-of-season squeeze" for spectacular savings on irregulars/damages. Here's how. If a store receives distressed irregular merchandise that's season specific, such as wool sweaters or cotton shorts, and it's nearing season's end (say the sweaters arrive in January), wait a week or two until the goods become extremely expendable to the store. You may profit from the cold selling climate.

▪ When dealing with a specific lot of merchandise, the difference between a good i.r. or distressed item and a bad one is this: Good finds have lesser flaws, but cost the same. An obvious truism, but keeping it in mind will stop you from scooping up the first "buy" you spot. Searching through the whole lot may secure you a spectacular specimen.

▪ You won't be able to return clothing captured through this outfitting strategy. It's sold as is, which is a one-way savings street. So take it to the checkout line only after checking it out from seam to shining seam. And trying it on, of course.

Suits designated i.r. deserve particularly careful scrutinizing. Some common problems, which you *don't* want to take on: "bubbles" of fabric in jacket lapels—they won't iron out; too-tight armholes; large creases, resembling folds, that don't go away when you put on a jacket (for example, you slip on a jacket and spot vertical creases around its armholes—these are caused by misplaced sleeves); sleeves that restrict your arm movement, or sleeves with creases or folds that don't go away when your arm is hanging in its normal position. As for pants, avoid i.r. designates with vertical folds of fabric around the front of the crotch. This is the effect of a misplaced zipper.

▪ You might not think fire-singed or smoke-soaked clothes could kindle a savvy wardrobe spark, but they often can. Obviously, if actually burned the garment is of little use. However, perhaps a shirt or sweater has only had its plastic wrapping melted. The goods may still be fresh.

As for smoke, there are two types of damage. Hot smoke permeates a garment's fabric and, fueled by a fire's heat, smoke odors can set. If you can see that an item has been cleaned, and it still smells strongly of smoke, leave it to smolder. Cold-smoke damage, on the other hand, is strictly surface stuff. It occurs when clothes are far enough away from a fire so that by the time smoke settles on them it has cooled to a granulated ash. This is usually removed with a vacuum cleaner by salvors, and smoke odors can be washed out.

▪ Water damage can cause mold, mildew, color bleeding, water marks, etc. But unless the garment's dye has been affected, or mold has really taken hold, most water damage will wash out. However, be wary of water-logged silks and fine linens and cottons; the more fragile a fabric, the more likely is permanent damage.

▪ Always consider having shopworn articles repaired. For example, missing buttons are probably the most common type of in-store damage. But they're easily and inexpensively replaced for an outlay that barely bites into your savings on tarnished apparel offering brilliant savings.

# Part II

# DRESSING SAVVY

# 8

# CAPITAL GAINS

## The Investment Dressing Option

THE FACT THAT we all put on pants one leg at a time doesn't mean much once they're zipped and people are looking at *them* to get a fix on what kind of person *we* are. Which is another way of stating the uncomfortable truism behind how-to-dress books: What we wear helps define who we are. We feel queasy admitting it. It seems to hint that great-looking clothes are glossy facades hiding lackluster people. Let's hope not. But we make conscious decisions—which do define us—to wear certain clothes. And *that* gives some weight to the "clothes make the man" school of thought.

If we enjoy dressing, this doesn't bug us. We sharpen our skills of wearable self-expression. We enjoy fine tuning our clothing's visual channel of communication.

The savings strategy outlined in this chapter, "investment dressing," approaches dressing with this in mind. It looks at the subject of how to dress better for less with more than the bottom line in mind. This strategy works best for men who understand clothing's intrinsic as well as apparent value and its ability to communicate on different perceptual planes. It's a dressing concept—actually many concepts—helping to define you in the very best way possible, and in the long run it can stretch your clothing dollars like golden rubber bands.

# Hidden Assets

You want to save some bucks and dress better, too. Why, then, would you *ever even* think of spending $475 for *any* single suit? Good question. Understand its answer and you've decoded investment dressing.

Most men have trouble justifying spending a lot on clothes. That's because quality in clothing isn't as readily apparent as in, say, a Mercedes-Benz or good golf clubs. It's more fair to compare menswear with something like abstract paintings, in that the quality of such paintings is often hidden if we don't know how to look at them. To illustrate this aspect of menswear, let's look at suits made by the Hickey-Freeman Company, the Mercedes-Benz of American suit makers. Perhaps no other name in business attire ranks higher.

The suits retail *starting* at about $475. Why so much? Non afficionados probably couldn't pinpoint it with a quick off-the-rack inspection. Sure, it looks as finely crafted as a Louisville Slugger or a Panasonic ten-speed, but so do a lot of clothes.

You have to look at what goes *into* the suit to realize its value. To help decode investment dressing, let's look at some of the construction details making Hickey-Freeman suits worth their high prices.

- The suits are made from the finest fabrics in the world. These pay off by being longer wearing and more resilient, so suits stay in shape and shed wrinkles. Plus, great fabrics sew better during construction, producing subtle shapes within a suit's silhouette where there would normally be flat, cardboardlike planes.

- While nearly all fabrics are delivered to suit manufacturers preshrunk, Hickey-Freeman subjects theirs to extra conditioning and finishing processes. Two advantages to this are extra richness added to a fabric's color and pattern, along with even more overall resiliency.

- Nearly all Hickey-Freeman suits are hand cut, one at a time. However, average suit pattern pieces (the kind used in making most designer goods) are cut with "saws" from fabric stacked more than a foot high. Hand cutting assures a precise matching of fabric patterns, and gives a more custom-tailored look.

- You've probably never seen "interlining" because it's the stiff inner fabric used to give suits shape and stiffness (such as in a lapel). In most suits, interlinings are "fused" in like iron-on T-shirt decals. In Hickey-Freemans, they're hand stitched into place, with about 1,200 stitches in the collar and lapels alone. This gives a suit pliancy, a soft, "human" shape.

- Forty-three separate pressings, plus a final pressing lasting more than an hour, is one of the most important hidden assets of a Hickey-Freeman. Repeated pressings smooth seams after sewing, creating clean, thin edges and seams. They also shape the garment during construction so it holds its shape, needs fewer pressings later, and assures the lines of the suit are locked in. Three or four years down the road it still retains its shape.

*Quality suits are bolstered by many unseen construction details, adding up to a noticeably better fit and look.*

*Investment dressing looks at clothing with more than the bottom line in mind.*

▪ The list goes on. Sleeves are shaped to follow the way your arm hangs when it's relaxed; about 1,300 feet of the finest silk thread go into the average suit; buttons are made from African and Asian water buffalo horn; zippers are nickel-plated brass.

The above "engineering report" isn't meant as an advertisement for Hickey-Freeman. The company doesn't need one. It's meant to show guys who can recognize quality in hamburgers or quality in beers or quality in tires that quality men's clothing has tangible value worth paying more for. Your average brand-name and designer clothing has some of it. Cheap clothes don't have any. You'll always have to think about investing in the best. But there are times, no matter how cash conscious you are, when such purchases can make sense. That's investment dressing in a nutshell.

## Shrink to Fit

Investment dressing is guided by a blue-chip credo easily embraced by all good cost cutters: Less is, if you know what you're doing, more. We implement this type of thinking when buying stereo equipment or toaster ovens. We spend a little more, the product lasts longer, and we enjoy it more. Same in menswear. If you buy one good suit instead of two cheapies, it will look good for a long time (unlike the cheapies, which never will) and you'll enjoy wearing it more.

Thus, sometimes saving money boils down to this: When you can't afford much, buy a few garments you like a *lot*, even if they cost a bunch. Then wear them with abandon. After years of steadfast service on their part, you'll have more than gotten your money's worth.

This doesn't necessarily mean getting by on a gold-plated, skeleton wardrobe. Once you've constructed a *core* of brilliant wearables, you supplement it with basic merchandise gleaned from implementing other savings strategies. The result of "less is, if you know what you're doing, more" thinking: luxurious style bought within a reasonable budget.

## Off Limits

Two reasons investors buy expensive IBM stock are that they know in five years IBM is going to be in business, and between now and then dividend checks are going to roll in like the tide. In menswear, good investments are wearable for years. And they pay dividends every time you put them on. Thus, a basic guideline to remember when spending big clothing bucks is to avoid the penny stocks, the trendy stuff, and go with steady styling.

Basically, this means avoiding the creative details by which designers earn their keep—the extra or snazzy buttons, zippers and patches, the pocket trim, all manner of tricky pockets, contrasting-color topstitching, etc., etc. Forget 'em. You're in an investment state of mind. You're going for sensibly tailored wardrobe additives that speak softly and carry a big kick, that will do so long after a cute pocket design bites the fashion dust.

Other general investment guides include buying your great goods in your best colors. The clothes will look even better on you, so you'll wear them more often. Also, for the most part, buy solids or small patterns. These are easier to wear and combine, and greater mileage increases your return on investment.

# Classic Act

It's a corollary to the "less is more" theorem, really, inescapable to the logical mind. The thinking man's buying guideline is, simply put, buy the conservative classics when buying the best. No other specific buying plan suits the overall investment-dressing concept better, for you can breed an impeccable closet stock if you're careful to corral and mate classic garments.

This is because the classics are the epitome of trend-eschewing clothes. You *know* you'll be able to wear 'em next year. Plus, if you play by the rules, which are well defined, building a core of investment-dressing classics is child's play. Last, the classics have a tendency to sustain supplemental purchases, serving as rock-steady counterpoints to most fashion trends.

# Best-Dressed Lists

Conservatism has been a fashion trend in menswear in recent years. So the classics have been merchandised, written and talked about until we might have felt like renegades if we didn't own a pair of khaki pants. Therefore, a cataloguing of traditionally blue-chip clothes may seem pat. Well, isn't that what the classics are all about? Here they are again. The for-sure styles, the banker's choice, the clothes you'd stake your job interview and weekends in the country on.

*Shoes:* Topsider deck shoes and moccasins, penny or tasseled loafers, wing tips.
*Shirts:* Button-down oxfords in white and blue. Polo shirts.
*Sportcoats:* Harris Tweed, cashmere, camel's hair.
*Blazers:* Navy, of course.
*Pants:* Khaki cotton pants, corduroys, blue jeans, gray flannel pants, white ducks. Plus khaki hiking shorts and solid white tennis togs.
*Suits:* Dark blue, gray flannel, tan poplin, blue pinstripes, gray pinstripes.
*Sweaters:* Cashmere V-necks, Shetland wool crew necks.
*Trench coats:* Burberrys, of course.
*Gloves:* Black leather, simpler the better.
*Umbrellas:* Black, with plain wooden handles.
*Briefcase:* Brown leather.
*Wallets:* Black or brown leather.
*Belts:* Simple black and/or brown leather.
*Tuxedos:* Traditional black dinner tux with grosgrain or satin lapels.

# More for Your Money

Time to rock the boat. Investment dressing on the classic track is safe banking, all right, *but*—was Picasso a classic painter? Does a Ferrari show the staid, sturdy lines of a BMW coupe? The point is, traditional classics are like granite, strong to build on, but to many eyes boring to look at. And when you spend big, you should get clothing that satisfies in a big way. If you only roam the classic corral, you'll never know the feeling of jumping its fence to gallop headlong into the wind. So some look for personal classics, and take the jump. After all, a Ferrari may be as well built as a BMW, but included in the purchase price is a walloping amount of design genius.

The Ferraris of fashion design, based mainly in Europe but dotting these shores, too, shouldn't be shelved without a fair reading. Sure, their clothes carry balloon-high price tags. And their reputations are based on the kind of inventiveness that looks silly on most of us. They're always using the newest ideas in fabrics, colors and silhouettes, but it's a misnomer to consider "fashion" off limits just because it's fashion. True, the trendy stuff, meant for trendies, is best left to them. Especially when novelty costs so much. But most European fashion reaching these shores isn't radical. Rather, it's an interpretation of contemporary menswear styling, using a distinctive fabric or color, and it's usually as tasteful as silver on white linen.

Thus, you can buy from the fashion innovators (names like Perry Ellis, Jhane Barnes, Giorgio Armani, Basile, Nino Cerruti, Gianni Versace and Valentino come to mind) within an investment-dressing scheme.

It just means jogging around fast-track fashion that's bound to burn out after a cometlike streak across fashion's horizon. Such meteoric lifespans occur most frequently in sportswear. There, an inexhaustible range of colors, fabrics, silhouettes and details provide too great a temptation for men and women who live to create landmark menswear. High-fashion designer *classics* show up most frequently in suits, sport coats and blazers, and dress pants. Here, there's not much room for gimmickry, and you'll know it when you see it.

For adventuresome wardrobe investors, then, one or two special garments per season from the fashion wizards form a core wardrobe. This is supplemented by classics or inexpensive "throwaway chic" items. On Wall Street this is called cost averaging. In such investment dressing, the only thing average is your closet size.

*Note:* Silk shirts are not considered traditional classics and needn't be innovatively designed to be special, yet they are the regular guy's quintessential investment-dressing purchase. A loosely cut crepe de chine shirt *looks* like bucks.

While building a core wardrobe is the most common form of investment dressing, building a core *accessory collection* takes another view. In this, expensive accessories (ties, belts, shoes, socks, jewelry, pocket handkerchiefs, etc.) are used

*Above, a crepe de chine silk shirt is one of the savviest looking investment-dressing purchases, but even a simple polo-style in rich cotton (left) can exude quality.*

to spark less expensive clothing collections. If this is your bent, consider such dramatic trappings as rich leather belts with sterling silver buckles, cowboy boots combining elegance with tough-skinned good looks, diamond and gold jewelry, watches that light up your wrist—marks of distinction casting big-buck looks.

## Breaking Up Is Hard to Do

Investment-dressing dollars can bring in more booty than just beautiful clothes you'll wear every time you get the chance. But you must tap a secondary savings supply line: versatility.

Makes sense, right? If you're buying an expensive tennis racquet it's nice if it has a big sweet spot along with blistering power. Well, when putting down the paycheck, it's nice to get something you can wear both during the day and in the evening, in the city or in the country, as well as anything with parts that can be worn separately.

An example of the day/evening, city/country garment would be a plaid shirt that could work with a gray flannel suit and a knit tie (day/city). But it could also work with a navy blazer and gray flannel pants (evening), and with a sweater on the weekends (country). Such a shirt would have to have a mild-mannered pattern and a color that could work for business. Now let's take that gray flannel suit. If it's the right type, and that will vary with the individual, you could take its pants and wear them with a tweed jacket or blazer. Or match the jacket, as a blazer, with some corduroy pants. The good ol' classics provide the most versatility, but it's found apart from them, too.

Since investment dressing implies working with a limited amount of clothing, versatility is closely related to clothing coordination, as the above example illustrates. In the end, a few good clothes working together make more sense than a closet full that mix like oil and water.

## Question Marks

Besides "is it versatile?", some other tough questions you should ask about investment garments while they're still on the rack are:

▪ Is this special purchase going to break into your wardrobe's starting lineup without necessitating a lot of other acquisitions to make it play well? If you have to buy new shoes, shirts and ties to make a suit work, think twice about buying it. It's more than the added purchases. The suit is likely to be "out of character" for you, or you would already own something to wear it with.

▪ Will you get enough opportunities to wear it to make it pay? A classy white dinner jacket may hit all the right notes, but if you can only wear it once a year, should you include it in your sartorial song? If a prospective purchase isn't in sync with your lifestyle it won't pay its way, either. For example, if you attend one or two formal occasions a year, is a pair of formal patent leather pumps needed?

▪ Do you like what you're getting? Sure, this sounds ludicrous, but if you're purchasing something because you think it's a good investment, and meanwhile it's leaving your nerve endings numb, you probably won't wear it enough to get your money's worth. A genuine fondness for something automatically increases its value to you.

▪ For more fashionable purchases, is its style reflective of a trend or a fad? Fashion trends affect the bulk of what's being sold in a given year; several years, in fact. The overall conservatism in suits during the late seventies and early eighties is an example. Fads, however, quickly pass. Pastel-colored pants, for example.

▪ Does the garment have quality? The *big question*. It deserves a thorough airing.

*A pair of quality shoes is a good base on which to build a core of investment-dressing wearables.*

# Well Built

"Quality is remembered long after the price is forgotten." Not a bad quote at all. Quality is the brass ring on the menswear merry-go-round. Grab it, and you feel you've done the best you can do for yourself.

Recognizing quality in clothes is essential no matter what dressing-for-less strategy you employ. The following guidelines could have fit in virtually any chapter in this book. They're included here for a couple of reasons. First, of course, is that when you're paying a great deal for something, every inch of it had better damn well exude quality. But a subtler reason is that some men go shopping, see something pricy, and think, Oh, for that price it must be good. Maybe yes, maybe no. So try to learn these quality checks. As alien as phrases in a foreign language now, after you use them for a while they'll become second nature.

• Use of a 100 percent natural fiber fabric in a garment is an indication of at least a certain level of quality. All-cotton, -linen, -wool and -silk are more expensive than synthetic or synthetic/natural blends, and for good reason. As you probably know, natural fiber fabrics are more comfortable to wear and they possess a *look* of quality. Unfortunately, they require more upkeep, and they wrinkle a bit more, but this often gives a garment a natural, relaxed appeal.

• Did you ever sustain a cut requiring stitches? If you did, you probably paid a lot of attention to how you were sewn back together. Did the doc do a neat job of it? Ask the same question when clothes shopping. Stitches should be neat. They should be even. They should be straight. Check along the waistbands of pants, around pocket edges and on a shirt's collar and cuffs. Small stitches usually make for stronger garments. For aesthetics, the thread's color should match the fabric's (transparent plastic thread is cheap).

• Fabric patterns such as plaids and stripes should shake hands at seams, meaning they should match up instead of clashing into one another.

• Generally, tightly woven fabrics hold up better than their looser counterparts, because threads have less room to shift and wear. Check on weave density by holding fabric up to light. The tighter the weave, the less light will penetrate. Of course, this applies only to unlined garments, and you have to take into account items like loosely woven cotton-knit sweaters, which don't come any other way.

• Some other quality giveaways: two rows of stitching under a shirt's armholes, for reinforcement; felt backing on the underside of jacket collars, to help retain the collar's shape; zippers lying flat and sewn in straight, that slide easily up and down their full length.

• Now look at seams (those running down pant legs and on the sides and shoulders of shirts, for example). They should be flat. The line formed where two pieces of fabric meet should be straight and thin. Puckered seams are the sign of a for-sure cheapie.

• Next, focus your attention on buttons and buttonholes. Buttons should button easily; buttonholes should have corners reinforced with thread. Quality tailoring makes for minimum fraying in and around buttonholes. Last, check for even spacing between buttonholes.

Since clothes aren't facades, it pays to look at their inner faces, too. There, a manufacturer shows his true quality consciousness. Here are some spot checks.

• The raw edges of fabric should be finished in some way. They're usually overstitched, although some have serrated edges, which are OK. Forget anything with raw, unraveling edges.

• A good tip-off to quality is the amount of extra fabric lavished on a garment. When inspecting the inside seams of pants, jackets and coats, look for at least ¼" of fabric on either side of the center seam, making alterations easier. (Especially at the back center seam in pants.)

There should be a good 1½" to 2" of extra fabric in the sleeves of jackets, to facilitate lengthening. (Along these same lines, 4" or 5" of extra fabric in the length of pants with unfinished hems indicate a manufacturer didn't cut corners.)

• Unfinished hems are themselves signs of quality. They indicate a manufacturer expects you'll want a perfect fit.

• A last look: Linings on suit jackets, sport coats and coats should be attached at one or two points at the bottom of the jacket or coat and at several points along side seams. A lining attached all around doesn't wear well. To see how a lining is attached, pull on it, from the bottom section, checking to see if it moves away from fabric underneath.

## Elite Fleet

An unsettling aspect of investment dressing is that the clothes used to make it work reside in retail stores where a dollar goes about as far as a balloon thrown into a stiff wind. Remember, we haven't been talking about national brands and designer lines you can pick up at most discounters. We've been talking crème de la crème. And the unfortunate fact is, this type of merchandise isn't found outside ritzy retailers'. Obviously, you'll try to find investment items on sale if you can, but this may mean paying $75 for a shirt that was $150.

This being the case, it's a good feeling to know that while the best menswear can cost a pot of gold, it doesn't cost a penny to walk into the very best clothing stores. And since frequenting ritzy retailers will likely be pocket-painful, it's best to view them as more than just storehouses of the right stuff. In fact, doing so can become as much a part of investment dressing as purchasing the most shining sartorial fare.

Look at it this way: The best stores are schools offering free courses in investment dressing. Sales help at better stores can guide you to the brands and designer lines best for you, and tell you why. It's like a waiter's ability to describe how a dish is prepared. In better stores, where sales help doesn't fluctuate every time a new school semester starts, salesmen get to know the qualities and drawbacks of the lines they sell, and how those lines relate to different types of customers. So when you make a substantial outlay on clothing you can know why it's worth the money.

Another aspect of quality retailers is their "private-label" goods. These are clothes the store has made up at a factory. Some stores simply have the factory sew a label (not necessarily the store's name) into the same merchandise that ten or twenty other stores carry with *their* labels. In these instances, private-label goods are basically vehicles used to get higher markups, the thinking being that since you have nothing to compare the merchandise to, you won't know that it isn't worth the price.

A better private-label system is when stores purchase their own fabrics and have a manufacturer sew up garments expressly for them. Stores contracting for such goods can pass some middleman savings on to consumers. How do you know if the private label is a good value? Stores have reputations to uphold and stores with great reputations aren't going to put their store name on an overpriced product. Therefore, if a store's name is in the garment, you may get good value, along with all the shopping amenities and services a great store offers.

## They've Got Your Numbers

Taken to one of its logical extremes, investment dressing leads to custom tailoring. If you're spending big, why not have some say in the matter, right? However, for most men this is just too great an expense. (Unless they make a Hong Kong connection—see chapter 3.) What can be an exception that pays off is made-to-measure shirts.

Made to measure means you get a custom fit, but a new garment pattern isn't made expressly for you, as in custom-tailoring work. And while such shirts cost $5–$20 more in the U.S. than when mail ordered from Hong Kong, the convenience and secure feeling of initiating a made-to-measure wardrobe here may be worth the extra money to you.

Buying made-to-measure dress shirts is investment dressing in a pure form, because while you're paying more, you're getting exactly what you want in exactly the right size.

What could be a better investment?

Many of America's leading menswear retailers offer made-to-measure services. So does the Custom Shop (716 5th Avenue, New York, NY 10019. 212-582-4366.

*Having made-to-measure shirts sewn up is investment dressing in pure form, because while you're paying more, you're getting exactly what you want in exactly the right size.*

Write for the location of the nearest of the chain's forty branches.) Costing from $25–$60, depending on the fabric used, the shirts differ substantially from ready-made varieties. Ready-mades are sized only by neck and a sleeve measurement. Made-to-measure shirts, however, are stitched up according to ten measurements, which are kept on file to facilitate reordering. There are three for the neck (circumference and two height measurements—one in front, one in back—which are then adjusted to the collar style ordered), as well as others for the arms and wrists (sleeves are sized to within one-half inch, cuffs are fitted to individual wrist dimensions). In addition, more measurements are taken for the waist, chest and torso. With made-to-measure shirts, you pick exactly the collar, pocket and cuff styles you like best from dozens of choices. And fabric swatch books contain hundreds of different fiber, pattern and color options. You may be asked to place a four-shirt minimum order. It's up to you whether such a litter is required, but four blue-chip stocks are better than ten flashy losers, right?

## The Price Is Right

Investment dressing is a many-faceted saving strategy. It's perhaps more a philosophy than any set of specific buying practices. After all, the very best pair of denim jeans costs under $30, and whether they constitute a special purchase seems to be an individual matter. Apart from that, bottom-line purists are likely to argue that clothes never elicit a more emotional response in them than, "It looks nice," and so will scrap the whole idea as a waste. Investment dressing, then, is a smaller concept than the sum of the clothes-buying strategies it encompasses, an outlook as much as a way of wardrobe enhancement.

# ▪ 9 ▪

# UNSEASONED VETERANS

## Building a
## Year-Round Wardrobe

MOST MEN'S WARDROBES are populated by part-time performers—wearables brought into action every six or eight months, but retired to storage after a quarter or half year's wear. Such shuffling is normal. It's the way we've been taught to put together and deploy wardrobes. What other way is there when the menswear on store shelves in June is as similar to the styles shown in September as dawn and midnight?

This "season specificity" is the modus operandi of menswear manufacturers and merchandisers. In turn, it's the way we've learned to buy clothes. It's not, however, the best way for the cost conscious to put together a cohesive wardrobe.

The total lack of congruity between menswear for the fall/winter season and that for the spring/summer is, in many ways, an outdated, unnecessary, wardrobe-wasting tradition. The tradition began many decades ago, when central heating and air conditioning were the dreams of men living beside fireplaces and under ceiling fans, when the weather outside had a nearly unimpeded impact on how comfortable we were inside.

Obviously, clothing producers would like to stick with tradition. It's difficult for them to think in terms of making clothes you can wear ten or twelve months out of the year, even when it's technically possible. After all, they stay solvent by motivating people to buy clothes. And if clothes are designed so they're only serviceable for six months at a stretch . . . well, you'll need two garments instead of one to get you through the solstices.

Now of course you need certain garments to keep the bones toasty when the cold winds blow and others to stop you from melting down when the sun shifts to "broil." But buying mostly season-specific clothes geared only to fall/winter or spring/summer is a real waste of closet space, not to mention your wallet's resources. And the drain on your money supply is quickened if you're the kind who runs in the latest style races, because wearing a garment for a few months out of the year, then discarding it after a couple summers or winters, drastically devalues your clothes-buying currency. In addition, it tends to nullify efforts at building a cohesive wardrobe.

Again, this doesn't refer to certain cold- or warm-weather essentials. You need them. But, if you want to build the most serviceable wardrobe possible, you also need to break the traditional cyclical squandering we've been taught to expect and accept. And you *can* circumvent this particular tyranny of tradition, because it's possible to cut way down on the number of season-specific clothes in your closet, substituting year-round wearables giving greater service. This allows you to decrease the number of clothes you buy, or lets you build a more extensive, more cohesive clothing corps that's always ready to hit the streets, either way running your clothes-buying dollars past costly seasonal limitations.

## Color Charting

One way to immediately start building a year-round wardrobe is to avoid "season-bound" color, a hallmark of season-specific wear. Designers usually chart their collections' color stories before actually sitting down at the design table. And while old designs and fabrics may be kept in a line, old color is always discarded for new. Why so much concern with color? Because it's readily identified by consumers as new, whereas a different fabric or design may not be.

But among the factors affecting how comfortable a garment keeps you, color ranks about as high as the type of buttons it sports. (OK, in the summer light-toned fabric reflects the sun, making for cooler composures. But other factors, such as a fabric's fiber content, weight and weave, are far more critical comfort-making characteristics.) There are, however, warm and cool hues, if you remember your color wheel, which manufacturers use in a seasonal coloring game. Basically, this game is played like this: For fall/winter, clothes receive deeper richer tone treatments; spring/summer wearables are made up in lighter tints.

The basis for these color changes is a bit outdated in itself. They're broadly based on the changes of season occurring in Northern latitudes, where the colors of foliage, as well as the intensity of light and shadow, shift dramatically every three months or so. But for the increasing number of Sunbelt residents in the U.S., such colors are not so much linked to their (your) environs as they are to—that's right—tradition.

How do you turn the color wheel in your favor for a wallet full of green and pocketfuls of silver? Two ways. One, instead of buying the deepest shades of fall/winter and the lightest tones cooked up for spring/summer wear, buy clothes in less season-specific hues. For example, "wine" is a perennial fall/winter color. But within the wine spectrum are deep, rich burgundies and lighter, fresher roses (or, continuing the wine theme, rosés). A burgundy is season-specific to fall. A rosé could go year round.

The other year-round color caper to count on in smashing season specificity is to buy truly seasonless colors. These include navy blue, gray, khaki and black. In addition, a tint like pink (as in shirts, not suits) is year-round in nature because few men wear it in any season.

There are specific strategies for combining colors in year-round wardrobes (to be discussed). But just choosing the types of colors mentioned above breaks the season-specific stranglehold and aids in putting together a cohesive, always-ready-for-wearing clothes collection.

# Cloth Bound

Like colors, menswear fabrics are seasonally shifted in a kind of aesthetic shell game, so that last year's materials are always as current looking as used napkins. Unlike tone and tint variations, however, a cloth's weave, weight and composition can spell clothing comfort.

Or discomfort. For again, many of the fabrics used today in menswear were developed decades or even centuries ago, when lifestyles differed from ours as radically as Harris Tweed differs from cotton-and-polyester knit—thus, the plight of the guy who wears his thicker-than-snowtires winter wool suit to a steam-heated office, or a rice-paper-thin linen shirt into a well air-conditioned work place.

Again, if you live in Minneapolis or Chicago or Buffalo or New York or Boston you're going to want a winter wool suit, no doubt about it. But should half your wardrobe be fashioned of "fall/winter" fabrics, the other of "spring/summer" materials? And if you live within the Sunbelt's balmy to hot-as-smoldering-charcoal climate, do you need a "winter" suit at all?

The necessity of making fall/winter clothes in fabrics entirely different from those used in spring/summer wear can be questioned. It isn't, though, because doing so rubs against every grain of the clothes-selling business. An example of this season-specific fabric thinking is corduroy's place in menswear. Consider this: corduroy pants are made of cotton, like denim jeans, and usually weigh less than their indigo counterparts. Denim jeans are worn year round, but corduroy pants can't be found in the stores after January or before August. Why? One reason is that corduroy has a ribbed, raised surface texture, which is considered a fall/winter characteristic. (Texture is a cold-weather fabric characteristic because fabrics for the cooler months are thick, allowing for raised dimensions.)

So stores stock *tons* of corduroy garments in the fall. But when those clothes sell out, retailers ban the ribbed, soft stuff from their shelves, instead showing clothes made of spring/summer-looking fabrics. A "fresh" store appearance, you know. Result: Corduroy is as entrenched as hot toddies as a cool-weather favorite—even though mid-weight corduroy could add cool clout to spring/summer garb, and serve as fall-wardrobe fodder as well.

## Weighty Issues

The fall/winter connotation of corduroy is the type of traditional bias you'll have to hurdle in honing a year-round wardrobe mentality. Others involve pegging a certain "fiber content" (the raw material from which yarn is spun, such as cotton, wool, silk, or synthetic fibers, like nylon) to a particular stretch on the calendar or, worse, eliminating certain fibers from specific seasons.

For example, most men think of wool as a summer scorcher. And cotton is a cold, as in freeze-your-butt-off, winter companion, right? Not necessarily. It depends on the weight (ounces per yard) and weave of fabric. Lightweight, thinly woven wool can be a cool summer fabric. Heavier weight, thicker cotton can make your winter warmer.

Given the same weight and weave, however, a garment's fiber content may be instrumental in determining how many months a year it can comfortably serve in your year-round regimen. In other words, certain fibers fit twelve-month wearing schemes better than others.

For example, in the right weight and weave, cotton is a good year-round fiber. It's good for cool weather because it's a hollow fiber that traps warm air. So it helps retain body heat. However, this hollowness allows cotton to absorb perspiration, and permits that perspiration to evaporate, helping your body's natural air conditioning do a good job in summer.

Wool is similar to cotton in its ability to be worn year round. (Again, if it's in the right weight and weave.) Why? Because wool fibers are twisted (imagine a spring made of hair). When these fibers are spun into yarn, natural air pockets trap warm air even better than cotton's hollow fibers. In summer, these allow perspiration to evaporate from the skin, albeit not as readily as does cotton, but readily enough if the wool fabric is light and thin.

So in a sense wool and cotton fluctuate in temperature with your skin. In contrast, such "solid" fibers as silks and man-made synthetics are not as obliging to those seeking year-round wearing from their clothes. These are "cold-blooded" fibers. They conduct air and perspiration about as readily as asbestos conducts fire.

*Lightweight, thinly woven wool sweaters make the comfort grade throughout the year.*

However, synthetic and silks are both easily blended with cotton or wool, making for fabrics giving service many months a year.

## Twelve-Month Tango

There's no such thing as a completely year-round wardrobe. Not many clothing pieces fit a twelve-month puzzle. But by avoiding season specificity, and by looking for optimum balance in regard to color, weight, weave and fiber, you'll minimize manufacturers' and retailers' "two-timing" tradition, saving bucks by utilizing the extra mileage delivered by year-round wearables.

Now for some specific garments and strategies to use in building a ten- to twelve-month wardrobe. Several examples of extended-use suits are available within the range of currently popular models. The best are made from "tropical" wools. These are 100 percent worsted wool fabrics weighing in at about 8 ounces per square yard (as opposed to winter-weight worsted suiting materials, which average about 12 ounces). Worsted wool is used in many quality men's suits. Unlike bulkier wool yarns, which are coarse and can itch, worsteds are tight and smooth, making for fabrics with a hard finish. Tropical worsteds are endowed with the good cool-weather qualities of wool fiber. But they're also light enough to take advantage of wool's summertime cooling qualities.

The suits most people think of when they think of year-round suits, however, are made of 55 percent Dacron/45 percent worsted wool. One reason for this is that, while worsted wool is a relatively expensive men's suiting material, Dacron/wool blends are some of the most reasonably priced. Another is that Du Pont-developed Dacron in the 1950s, when men's suits generally weighed much less than today's

Some year-round *wearables* are, *clockwise from top left:* mid-weight corduroy suits, long-sleeved cotton polo shirts, cotton sweaters, trench coats and Dacron-and-wool blend suits.

models. Thus, the company wanted a synthetic fiber that would blend easily with lightweight worsted wools, and so developed Dacron specifically for the worsted yarn spinning system. While blended Dacron and wool doesn't offer the luxury of tropical worsteds, it makes for durable, inexpensive, easy-care suits steeped in year-round readiness.

Wool gabardine suits should be another pick for men nurturing wardrobes to deliver twelve-month service. The fabric is of a hard-wearing twill construction (the same weave used in denim), so "gab" suits take year-round wear on the chin while still delivering knockout style punches. Rounding out the extended-wear suit lineup are corduroy ensembles in 8–10 ounce material, and a corduroy suit's jacket and pants can be worn separately, further stretching serviceability. As with any items you're looking to wear throughout the year, suits accumulated in the basic colors of navy (solid and pinstripe), gray (solid and pinstripe), khaki and perhaps black, have any-month appeal.

Most dress shirts are year-round in nature. However, those in the popular batiste cotton or voile weaves are strictly summer oriented, and are better stocked in minimum quantities. Broadcloth is the perfect medium-weight weave, while oxford cloth is a bit heavier. Both, however, are shoo-ins for twelve-month roles.

## Pileup

While putting together a year-round suit/dress shirt grouping is relatively easy, just finding twelve-month sportswear is tough. It's as if designers heap on every seasonally entrenched color and fabric in the book when creating fall/winter and spring/summer sportswear lines. Deep, rich colors and inch-thick fabrics here, wispy textiles and pastel colors there—the middle ground is easily lost in such creativity.

One solution to this problem is to pepper your closet with the few seasonless sportswear items around, then stretch the shirts and sweaters from this group into the cooler months, letting them serve double duty, and letting you put a freeze on expenditures for cool-weather wearables.

This involves layering lighter weight tops for warmth. The method works, because by layering garments you trap warm air, and such heated-air buffers around the body act as great natural insulation. Some items that might be put to such use are long-sleeved polo shirts, sweat shirts, turtleneck sweaters and light-weight denim shirts. For example, you might wear a long-sleeved polo shirt under an oxford cloth button-down, with a cotton crew neck sweater over the two. Such a pileup would take you well into cooler months, yet its ingredients could be worn throughout the spring and summer as well.

## Multiple Choice

Of course, the concept of layering can only be the top half of the season-less sportswear strategy. You can't wear a pair of cords over a pair of jeans, right? Right. But fortunately, corduroy, denim, and cotton sweat pants, as well as cotton chinos, and lightweight wool weaves (gabardine, wool crepe and tropical wools) can pull ten- to twelve-month duty.

## Into The Trenches

Other seasonless clothes are hard to come by. But there's one item offer-ing the type of serviceability you should be looking for. It's the trench coat. The traditional, and perhaps quintessential extended-wear garment. Incorporating a trench in your wardrobe, instead of the two or three items needed to fill its void, is a year-round wardrobe strategy streamlined with the kind of saving savvy needed to cut costs without cutting corners.

Some of the first men to discover what extended-wear dressing was all about were the British officers of WWI. Upon checking into their hotel rooms, they would unbutton the wool linings from their Burberry trench coats to use as bathrobes. Today, the trench's multifaceted service record continues. The classic trench, with its cotton or wool gabardine shell and wool button-in lining, may be the only coat you'll ever need. In spring the shell is a raincoat. In fall a lightweight warmer. In winter, button-in wool lining in place, the design delivers overcoat warmth. Now that's extended wear.

The idea of multiplying a garment's usefulness by using a zip- or button-in liner and/or detachable sections is being incorporated into a number of contemporary designs, for example, down jackets with zip-off sleeves, which shed to leave a vest, or "bush pants" with zippers at mid-thigh, letting you switch from trousers to shorts with a flick of the wrist. Using such extended-wear clothing items helps nix your wardrobe's season-specific nature.

## Monthly Planners

As mentioned, there's no such thing as a completely year-round wardrobe. The best you can hope to do is lessen the number of clothes giving sporadic service. You probably wouldn't want a completely year-round wardrobe, anyway. For if one of the things you buy clothes for is pleasure, some shift in the garments offered for fall/winter from the ones presented for spring/summer is pleasurable. In other words, change can be, as you've no doubt discovered, exciting.

Putting together a year-round wardrobe, then, is an attempt to control change, not banish it, a set of strategies letting you decide why you'll wear a certain color, fabric or design. A last example of how you might incorporate such control into your wardrobe when thinking in a year-round way involves dress shirts and suits.

Because most dress shirts are year-round by nature and most suits are season specific, the way you probably put them together now is to wear most of your dress shirts with both your fall/winter and spring/summer suits. Most dress shirts aren't season specific in color, so there's no problem with this. In fact, it's the way the clothing business has traditionally been set up.

But a recent development has opened up the possibility of dressing differently for men seeking year-round wear—and variety—from their clothes, the development of "designer" shirts, which are as season specific as any menswear items.

Why would you want to mess with such obvious attempts at color-chart maneuvering?

Because shirts are cheaper than suits. And because shirts don't change weight with the passing months, so you could conceivably wear them year round, even if

*Buying such extended-wear clothing items as jackets with button-in liners
helps nix your wardrobe's season-specific nature.*

the colors didn't match the calendar. In such a scheme, instead of changing your
suits with seasonal regularity, you would switch shirts and ties. You would buy
your suits in tropical worsted wools, Dacron/wool blends, gabardine and corduroy.
You would acquire them in the seasonless colors of navy blue, gray, khaki and,
possibly, black. You would also have on hand a navy blue blazer in tropical
worsted wool (one year-round garment many men already take full advantage of),
which could easily be worn with the pants from the gray or khaki suits.

Then, in the fall, you would wear dress shirts and ties incorporating vibrant,
deep colors—for example, a white shirt with wine, dark brown and green stripes,
worn with a wine-colored tie. In spring, these accessories would lighten up—for
example, a yellow shirt worn with a turquoise tie. Such a strategy couldn't completely replace the suit/shirt/tie arrangements now ruling your closet order, but a
partial commitment to such a scheme would extend your wardrobe's and wallet's
riches.

# 10

# ORIGINAL EQUIPMENT

## Active Wear
## as Street Wear

SPORTS.

Clothing designed specifically for sports.

Clothing "borrowed" from sports for use in everyday life.

That, in short order, is how athletic wear trickles down to become part of "normal" menswear. It also pinpoints a sporting savings strategy making for winning casual-wear looks.

The plan: Obtain inexpensive, tough-hewn clothes originally designed for active sports, such as sweat pants, sweat shirts, gym shorts, soccer jerseys, etc. The action: Wear them as casual street wear. The result: a beefed-up wallet in prime savings shape.

## Active Influence

Until recently this was about as good an idea as eating leaves to cut your food bills. As little as six or seven years ago, you wouldn't wear gym shorts on bigcity streets. But then something called sports and fitness happened in a very big way. The fitness boom was bound to converge with men's fashions, because designers latch on to new lifestyle trends and interpret them faster than anyone. And clothes don't hang on walls, they hang on bodies, so guys spending three or four hours a week toning up their body architecture are bound to want to dress it differently than before. With the onrush of bicycling, tennis, jogging, etc., designers have begun making clothes for healthy, athletic, young-minded men.

*Polo shirts originated in response to the specific requirements of a sport, but have since made the transition to classic casual attire. Today, matching polos with sweat pants is but one active-as-street option.*

*Left, authentic rugby jerseys and sweat pants are two active-as-street star players.*

To design for this new type of man, the people who make men's clothing are dipping into the wellspring of ideas flowing from clothes originally designed for sports, translating the ideas incorporated in functional sports clothing into street wear. The influence of sports and fitness is dramatically seen in casual sportswear, where bright colors and body-conscious shapes (those incorporating the body or its natural outline into the overall design) are now the norm.

All this fashion evolution has set the stage for a particularly eighties savings strategy. While it used to be strange to wear inexpensive clothes designed for active sports on the street, today doing so accomplishes one of two things: It bypasses designer interpretations of the real thing, or it inexpensively substitutes for more expensive traditional sportswear. In either case, it's putting the dollar saving thrill of victory on your back.

The bottom line is that authentic active wear costs much less than either the designer knockoff versions of it or its traditional casual-wear counterparts.

## Sports-Minded

You very likely already have a foot and torso in the active-wear-turned-street-wear savings plan. No? Well, take a look in your closet locker and see if you don't find a pair of sneakers and at least one polo shirt.

Sneakers and polo shirts. Two winning examples of the active-as-street concept. Two pioneers in the transition of active apparel from fields and courts to sidewalks and living rooms.

Sneakers made the leap first, demonstrating that the right sports gear could muster mass appeal. First fashioned in the 1860s, original versions boasted rubber soles, canvas uppers, and laces—all the details recognized as standard equipment on our own sneaks. Designed as a rich man's croquet shoe, they were labeled "croquet sandals," and sold for a whopping $6. But the idea was too good to putter around well-groomed lawns for long. In only five years, hoards of working men, who had gripped about as many croquet mallets in their lives as they had $1,000 bills, were ordering sneakers from the Sears catalogue for 60 cents. The soft, sporty footwear has been a wardrobe staple ever since. Today they're so *commonplace*, yet they originated as sports gear.

Polo shirts clearly show the active-to-street transition, in which garments originate in response to the specific requirements of a sport, but then, like a star quarterback who lands a job in the sportscasting booth, are led to victory off the field as normal attire.

Polos were the first modern clothes designed for a particular sport. The design permitted a polo player to maneuver his charging mount and take his shots with physical abandon. The shirt was so comfortable it was adapted to golf and tennis wear. But, more important, men soon wore it away from the links, courts and polo grounds, making a sports-generated top into a sport-shirt staple. And recently, as you know, polos have been more popular than low-salt diets, making their move to casual wear not only complete, but overwhelming.

## It's the Zeal Thing

Today, a whole batch of garments is lined up behind sneakers and polo shirts, just itching to break into the street-wear leagues. And savvy savers are giving them lots of playing time. Some, in fact, trust whole segments of their casual clothing to active-as-street clothes. Their closets are stocked with sweat pants, sweat shirts, sleeveless sweat shirts, cutoff sweat pants, gym shorts, tank tops, T-shirts and other active apparel. And that's it for leisure wear.

Any such zealotry, of course, tends to trap practitioners, though in this case it's a cushy cage. But such enthusiasm points up the incredible "rightness" the active-as-street savings strategy offers many men today. It's a new kind of dressing, 1980s born and bred, because it is *lifestyle* rather than fashion oriented. These days most men want comfortable clothes, and active-as-street is as comfortable and casual as lounge chairs. Most styles are cut simply and loosely, allowing the kind of movement competition spurs and relaxation welcomes. (Some people term active-as-street no-sweat dressing, alluding to the role sweat shirts and sweat pants play in it, but also to the ease with which active-as-street clothes are worn.)

You're not likely to trash your jeans, khakis, cords, etc., for a batch of sweat pants, but it's hard to imagine not finding a place for no-sweat dressing in your sartorial scheme. It's too practical a money saving alternative.

# Tough Team

The garments playing point positions in active-as-street are champs, tested in competition, constructed to hang tough on and off the field, often ignited by a gamut of gladiatorlike colors. Here are some of the best.

▪ Tank tops and gym (or basketball) shorts are, of course, staples. They're cool, comfortable, simple—what more can be said? One thing: The "New Zealand" style running shorts with overlapping but unsewn side seams are a movement improvement over the original design.

▪ Sweat shirts and sweat pants are also fashioned in the form-follows-function mode. How have these unassuming pull-ons come to cover so many, even après exercise? Maybe it's because they're the closest thing to Levi's and T-shirts yet invented. Comfortable. Adaptable. Absolutely no sweat to wear.

▪ Menswear manufacturers have borrowed details and, in many cases, pirated complete looks from soccer and rugby. It's easy to see why. These clothes possess the biggest, boldest color kick around, along with eminently street-suitable style.

▪ Baseball shirts and jackets, styles which have also contributed their share of inspiration to casual-clothing manufacturers' lines, can also hit street-savvy homers outside ball parks.

▪ The many jerseys available (hockey, motorcycle motocross, soccer, football, wind surfing, etc.) epitomize tough-natured, inexpensive active wear. Constructed like work wear, they'll thrive on the type of abuse sending designer creations into retirement. They endure repeated washings as if practicing swimming strokes. Many are priced to appeal to budget-minded schools and sports teams. Long-sleeved all-purpose jerseys, for example, range from $8–$15, depending on size and fabric content.

▪ Bicycling gear is a casual-clothing alternative, but points up how authentic active wear can be "activity bound." The problem is, hard-core cycling gear hugs the body as if pasted on. That's fine for those endowed with Nautilus-perfect or thin bodies. On a normal build, though, it can be unflattering street wear.

▪ Boxing gear is usually limited to the cooler months. That's when such tough stuff, made of cotton-backed wool and intended to make fighters sweat during workouts, delivers its best punch.

*Boxer's training trunks deliver functional no-frills fashion on a budget; soccer shoes are similarly rough and style ready.*

*Right, soccer jerseys, rugby shorts, and soccer socks and shoes give street wear an active kick.*

## Sturdy Savings

When putting yourself in the active-as-street game, remember that authentically active gear runs a different race than traditional clothing. Usually this wins you a lot of style points. But sometimes it takes some getting used to.

For example, while there are numerous all-cotton and a few all-wool active styles around, many clothes born to play the field are made of steely synthetic and synthetic-blend fabrics. This can be a sign of inferior quality in conventional clothes, which look better in all-natural materials. However, synthetics strengthen sports-generated clothing's position as easy-care wear, keeping in top shape even when abused and washed repeatedly.

You'll come across fiber mixes like 75 percent polyester/25 percent nylon. Purists will argue synthetics lack aesthetics when compared to the naturals. But that's missing the point. Functionalism supplants subtler values in active wear.

On the plus side of the scorecard, synthetics and synthetic blends are time and money savers, being easier and cheaper to maintain. While synthetic/blended fabrics are not very luxurious in look or feel, this is compensated for in active sports stuff by bright colors and solid detailing, adding up to visually exciting garments.

Added to natural fibers, synthetics can combine good points from each fiber type. For example, polyester/cotton and polyester/wool blends are stronger and more wrinkle resistant than 100 percent cotton or wool. Rayon blended with cotton adds strength and luster. Acrylic blended with cotton produces softness, greater crease resistance, shrink resistance, faster drying, and minimum ironing.

Of the pure synthetics, silky, slippery knitted nylon and rayon are stretchable, colorfast, shrink resistant, strong as wire (well, almost), lightweight, extremely washable and quick drying. Nylon tricot, used in much active apparel, is extremely lightweight and durable, yet never needs ironing.

## Scoring Points

Active-as-street is as much a way of dressing as a way of obtaining clothes for less. It's sweat pants worn with polo shirts; tennis or gym shorts worn in lieu of walking shorts; soccer, rugby, football and other jerseys worn with casual slacks.

Running this type of outfitting a few yards further down the sartorial field (and this is already being done by a number of men), wear brightly colored cotton sweat shirts in lieu of crew neck sweaters, or wear a softly constructed blue blazer over a sweat suit. You get the picture.

## Source Spots

Wearing active-as-street is a savings strategy easily implemented, and one made all the more enjoyable by getting the best deal on your active wear. Sporting-goods shops are the biggest sources, but not necessarily the least expensive. The best bargains on the sporting scene come from setting your savings spotlight on athletic apparel manufacturers selling directly to the public. Here are some that sell through the mail.

SOCCER SPORT SUPPLY (1745 First Avenue, New York, NY 10028. 212-427-6050) offers the best in soccer and rugby clothes at incredibly reasonable prices. They manufacture many of their wares and sell directly to the public. (They supply many professional soccer teams across the country as well.) Some of the most stylish soccer offerings are short- and long-sleeved soccer jerseys sporting team logos from Holland, West Germany, Brazil, Italy, England, the U.S., Scotland, Poland, Argentina or Ireland, plus Real Madrid, Hamburg or Liverpool (about $17.50 for short sleeves, $19.50 for long).

Colorful professional-style soccer pants also make the winning grade in 100 percent cotton (about $7), 100 percent nylon (about $6.25) and 100 percent extra-heavy nylon knit (about $8.50). Soccer jerseys in the brightest colors and stripes, with several different collar designs, range from $11 to $16 (a steal).

Rugby apparel is perhaps the toughest around. Soccer Sport's authentic international rugby jerseys are crafted of 100 percent "super-heavyweight" English knitted cotton, featuring all triple-stitched seams, untearable twill collars with rubber buttons, underarm reinforcement gussets and extra-reinforcement at all stress points (from about $21–$26). Also available are "real strong" imported rugby pants of 100 percent drill cotton, with two front pockets, elastic hip sections, fly front and drawstring waist (about $16). There is a $10 minimum, plus shipping and handling charges, on all orders.

G & S SPORTING GOODS (43 Essex Street, New York, NY 10002. 212-777-7590) makes its own boxing and general athletic wear, selling to boxing clubs and, by mail order, to individuals. In their bare-bones price sheet, you'll find such sports-specific items as "top-grade satin boxing trunks with contrasting waistband and side strips" (about $7).

But more easily adaptable training gear is ready to hit the road, too. Examples are the cotton-backed wool training trunks in short, knee and full (ankle) lengths, all with adjustable drawstring waists (about $10, $13 and $16, respectively), and to match them, sleeveless cotton-backed wool tank tops (about $10).

White terry cloth belted boxing robes are easily housebroken (about $19, or $26 with hood). Basic hooded cotton sweat shirts (about $11) and cotton draw-string-waist sweat pants (about $8) are value priced too.

*Professional-style soccer shorts in a variety of bright colors can play the field as street wear, too.*

*Substituting for the traditional sweater and pants, a sweat suit adds an active dimension when worn under a blazer.*

Sportswear Clearinghouse (Box 173-W4, Winchester, MA 01890) bills itself as a liquidator, buying up leftover stocks from retailers and manufacturers at below wholesale, and passing the savings on to you. Because the stock here is always shifting, you'll have to write to see what's available at any one time.

The Finals (21 Minisink Avenue, Port Jervis, NY 12771. 800-431-9111) is, as its free catalogue says,

> The largest team supplier of racing swimwear in the United States. In only six years, we've grown to be #1, but until now only important swimmers have been able to take advantage of our fast service, high quality, and low inflation-fighting prices. . . . We're able to keep our prices so low because we offer our products by mail, and ship them direct from our factory. We've eliminated the middleman and his profits have become your savings.

The Finals direct-to-you method offers such deals as a "Repeats" 100 percent Antron nylon swim brief, a "durable, comfortable, noncompetition suit for lap swimming or lounging" for about $7. Other in-the-swim savings include swim caps (about $1.50) and sun visors (about $3–$5). The supplier's line of gym shorts and boxer-style stretch-knit swim trunks starts at about $7, their cotton and polyester polo shirts go for about $12, or three for $33.

Camp Beverly Hills (9615 Brighton Way, Beverly Hills, CA 90210. 213-202-0069) is the philosophical leader of no-sweat dressing in the United States. Begun as an army surplus/vintage clothing store, the operation has packaged the active-as-street look into a chic, California lifestyle oriented hipness. A spokesman for the company comments:

> The success of this look is based on peoples' lifestyles. For example, on the old show, "You Bet Your Life," with Groucho Marx, they would always pan the studio audience with the camera, and you'd see every guy in a suit and tie and every woman would be wearing hats and gloves. That was in the 50's. Now look around. You see guys in supermarkets wearing sweat suits. Dressing is just changing. It's getting more casual. Once you get used to being comfortable in your clothing, it's very hard to go back.

The Camp Beverly Hills catalogue is a veritable active-as-street textbook, as well as a fun-to-read guide offering over fifty value-priced items. Lots of sweat shirts (long, short and cutoff models), sweat pants, jerseys, baseball jackets, gym shorts, socks, shoes, etc., in California-bright colors.

# Post-Game Wrap-Up

Like any new way of dressing, active-as-street is being spawned by the times. Whether it will flourish in the future remains uncertain. Now, however, this savings strategy offers a fast track to casual wardrobe savings.

# 11

# WORKING-CLASS HEROES

## Uniform Companies' Sturdy Savings

CEMENT-STRONG wardrobe workers, "blue-collar" clothes deliver as much casual sartorial service as menswear priced twice as high. Making up the blue-collar ranks are styles that haven't been laid off in decades—the type of burly coverings worn by construction workers, telephone linemen and bottled-gas deliverers for generations. Such unchanging, no-frills styling, combined with the ability to take a truckload of abuse, provides a wear worthiness spanning years instead of seasons, and today a warehouse full of work wear is ready to clock out from garages and packing rooms into more relaxed surroundings.

In addition to blue-collar clothing, work wear in the form of professional and service uniforms is ready to walk off the job into a street-savvy career, too. Styled for well-delineated roles, such clothes as waiter's jackets and doctor's "operating room" smocks and pants can fill specific wardrobe niches, if adroitly employed, and for far less money than "normal" street attire.

Coming right up: how work wear can muscle into your closet as street garb, and later, the saving graces of professional and service uniforms.

## Work Record

Few other clothing genres have contributed as many specific styles to mainstream menswear as clothes originally designed for the working man. In this respect blue-collar garb is like military clothing or active sportswear.

And just as bomber jackets are worn by men who would rather take the train than a 727, clothes originally worn by lumberjacks are donned today by guys filling their quota of daily physical labor by taking out the trash.

The first transitions of clothing from work to play involved the cold-weather garb worn by laborers at the century's turn. At the time, only men like lumberjacks, construction workers and telegraph linemen, who earned their keep building America, required extra-sturdy cold combatants. Men who worked inside chose "normal" winter coats and sweaters to keep warm.

But change was in the offing, a consequence of WWI's big bang. One outcome of the war was the new clothing sensibility instilled in doughboys, who got used to the functional ease of their uniforms. When they came home, many civilian styles seemed as loose and comfortable as wearable cardboard. But one group of clothes was more to their liking: work wear.

And all of a sudden there was a new need for sturdy, casual clothing. Before the war, a huge percentage of working men were physical laborers, with little time for pure recreation. Afterward, more white-collar jobs opened up, and with them came the relatively new commodity of leisure time, along with the need for new clothes to wear while enjoying it.

Today we take ski jackets, down vests, hiking boots and the rest of the modern rugged-wear corps for granted. Seventy years ago nothing like it existed. It was born out of work and military styles.

By the mid-1920s college students took to wearing bold-checked red-and-black lumberjack shirts and sheepskin vests, both strictly work-wear items in their grandfathers' day. As it turned out, it wasn't the last time students turned on to work wear. The same phenomena in the sixties spawned the blue-jeans revolution. Originally worn by cowboys and construction workers, jeans represent work wear's biggest splash in mainstream menswear to date.

Indigo jeans, shirts and jackets are the most ubiquitous examples of onetime work wear now hanging out on the streets. But others abound. For example, carpenter's pants, chamois cloth and flannel shirts, overalls, lumberjack shirts and "work" boots are accepted casual-wear styles, and all were recruited for street service from work wear's ranks.

Today, those ranks are filled with other styles ready to put in long hours of casual-clothing service. Because so much blue-collar clothing is already walking the bridge from work to play, wearing more of the real thing is a bit of sartorial boundary crossing that's one of the simpler routes to dollar-wise clothing rewards.

And when it comes to delivering more wear for the money, few clothes get the job done as well. Several price breakers keep costs at a level any man who must bring home the bacon to put a shirt on his back can appreciate.

## Style Set

One reason today's work wear is priced so low is that it tends to succumb to fashion trends about as readily as glaciers melt in Antarctica.

"We don't sell fashion items. We sell commodities, which have a long shelf life," said a spokesman of the Eastern Wear-Guard Company, the nation's largest supplier of work clothing and industrial uniforms. Eastern claims to serve over 350,000 companies nationwide, but individuals may also order from their large catalogue. (Write Eastern Wear-Guard, P.O. Box 400, Hingham, MA 02043. Catalogue free.) "Not having to worry about the clothes going out of style at the end of a season helps us offer low prices. For example, we've sold some of the basic styles for more than twenty years. And since we're making the same garments year in and year out, we don't have to change our patterns or invest in designers. It all helps keep prices down."

Eastern manufactures most of the garments they sell, and since most designs are set in sartorial stone, they can buy huge quantities of fabric at reduced rates, increasing their factory-to-you savings, which they claim are 10 to 30 percent lower than retail.

*Blue-collar work wear is priced about half as high as mainstream menswear.*

Eastern's prices are about a half to a quarter of department-store tariffs. But the merchandise isn't comparable. Lack of current styling isn't the only difference. As the marketing manager for Eastern put it, "It's a different kind of value."

For example, basic pants, twill shirts, jump suits (coveralls) and jeans are available in 100 percent cotton. But the majority of work-wear items are fashioned for easy upkeep, and that means polyester-and-cotton blended fabrics. Thus, prices are extremely reasonable, but most of the clothes can't compete on the aesthetic level with name-brand or designer goods. "The clothes are designed with a full cut for people to work in. And they're designed to last a long time and stand some abuse. But some are not at all stylish," summed up Eastern's spokesman.

Such an uncompromising commitment to sturdy blandness isn't necessarily bad. After all, that's one of work wear's great attractions. For example, many styles carry extra-heavy-duty zippers and reinforced seam stitching. As for the clothing's "uncommitted" fit, it's a double-edged style sword.

It's a boon to men who find wearing designer jeans as comfortable as being stuffed into a car trunk. Shirts are full, because guys working in warehouses and garages want to be able to move around unencumbered. Pants are similarly designed. With a longer rise (a.k.a. more room in the crotch) than most current dress or sport slacks.

Such un-body-conscious cuts mean you can't count on these clothes for quick fashion injections. You have to apply the proper aplomb. In other words, the savings are there, the style is up to you.

## Switch in Time

Work-wear designs may change about as fast as the shape of oil drums, but a big change in the concept of blue-collar garb vs. mainstream clothing is creating more varied savings opportunities for men looking to employ labor-oriented retailers and mail-order merchants in their dress-for-less game plan.

In this turn of events, "normal" casual styles, such as polo shirts and nylon baseball jackets, are entering work wear's realm. Thus, many suppliers of working men's working wardrobes are stocking these items, for far less than regular retailers.

Another shift: Up until the general demolition of dress codes in the 1960s (brought about in part by the casual tide of blue jeans flowing into mainstream menswear), almost all uniforms were sold in solid, matching colors. Today, more variety prevails. For example, ten years ago, only solid-colored pants and shirts were sold as uniforms, such as navy blue pants with matching navy shirt. Today, navy blue pants may match up with a light blue or blue-and-white striped top. Such variation further expands your work-wear procurement options.

## Assembled Line

While uniform retailers today may sell anything from lumberjack shirts to jogging outfits, some styles are standard. Such basic work wear is sold at department stores like Sears and Penneys, as well as discount department stores like K-Mart. More styles are likely to be had from specialized dealers, who can be found in the Yellow Pages under Uniform Suppliers. Following are some examples from Eastern Wear-Guard's catalogue:

Long-sleeved, extra-durable 100 percent cotton twill shirts in navy or light blue, about $16.

Matching navy blue pants in 100 percent cotton twill, about $19.

A 100 percent cotton jump suit is billed as "one of the toughest garments ever made." Sporting six pockets, the suit is made of a heavyweight fabric in an interesting herringbone weave. About $32.

A "20 below" thermal insulated vest incorporating three pockets features a nylon shell and is filled with Dacron 88 Hollofill "for maximum warmth and minimum weight." About $14.

"Heavy-duty work jeans" are battle readied with side tool pockets and loops and reinforced at stress points. About $17.

Chino pants in cotton-and-polyester twill, about $18.

## Career Converts

While most professions can claim to have their own language, few can boast their own clothing styles. However, physicians and waiters utilize specialized work wear you can take to the streets. Their garb cannot be as diffusely deployed as hard-core blue-collar styles, but under certain circumstances it makes for nearly matchless alternatives to mainstream styles and prices.

The two most street-worthy styles of physicians' apparel are "operating room" (or O.R.) all-cotton smocks and drawstring pants. Standard colors are jade green and white. Both garments fit loose and easy, making for supreme summer wear. The smocks are styled with V-necklines, short cap sleeves and single breast pockets. The pants sport a drawstring waist, adding to their comfort.

Worn together, or separately, they incorporate the most comfortable characteristics for summer dressing. O.R. smocks and pants are available for about $12 and $14, respectively, from Bencone Uniforms (121 Carver Avenue, Westwood, NJ 07675. Catalogue free).

The waiter's profession can offer a solution to the problems of a man seeking alternatives to costly yet so seldom-worn tuxedos. The plan: Instead of a tux investment, procure a waist-length waiter's jacket. These are available in a variety of fabrics, designs and colors from shops specializing in restaurant uniforms (in the

The waiter's profession offers a solution to the problems of a man seeking alternatives to costly yet seldom-worn tuxedos. Substituting for a tux is the waist-length waiter's jacket, available from restaurant uniform suppliers.

Below, the two most street-worthy styles emerging from physicians' specialized apparel are "operating room" (or O.R.) all-cotton smocks and drawstring pants, in the standard colors of jade green and white.

Yellow Pages under Uniforms-Restaurants, if you live in a large city). Worn with dress pants, these jackets achieve the high-fashion short tux jacket look on low-budget terms.

To dress them more formally, purchase a cummerbund and, of course, a bow tie. A wing-collar tuxedo shirt is optional if attending less formal fancy affairs, de rigueur for black tie. If such jackets are not available in your city, try Scafati, Inc., "manufacturers of fine uniforms and formal wear" (260 West 41st Street, New York, NY 10036. Write for ordering information). Scafati sells polyester, Dacron/rayon and all-wool short waiter's jackets for about $30, $42 and $75, respectively, which, as with most work-wear styles, is certainly less sweat off your wallet's back compared to the current cost of mainstream menswear.

# ▪ 12 ▪

# CORPORATE POSTURES

## Clothing
## as a Tax Deduction

IF YOU SUIT UP for work every day, with shirt, tie and all the trimmings, chances are your business garb accounts for most of your clothing expenditures. But you're willing to foot a big workday wear bill. After all, we're talking about the armor in which you challenge the world—climbing equipment for scaling the success ladder.

Until recently there wasn't a way to circumvent the cost of office attire besides smart shopping. Today, businessmen may be able to erase 50 to 80 percent of the red ink business wardrobes generate. How? Through "corporate clothing programs," in which companies buy business wear for employees. A relatively new concept, the plans are tailored for men wishing to perfect business wardrobes while protecting clothing budgets.

The idea originated in England as a perquisite, or perk. Perks are noncash compensations given employees in order to let them avoid higher tax rates. (In Great Britain, high taxes wipe out many of the benefits of high salaries.) In the U.S. fewer corporate clothing programs are instituted as perks. Most are begun to patch up or fine tune a company's corporate image. But if you can get into such a plan, the benefits are the same: huge savings on the clothes you wear to bring home the bacon.

## Give and Take

Exactly how do corporate clothing programs work? Under such arrangements, corporations buy employees business wardrobes from retail stores or

*Corporate men in a 50 percent tax bracket would pay $800 in pretax income to buy a $400 suit. If part of a corporate clothing program, however, they would only pay $200 (or $400 in pretax income) in taxes on the same suit.*

**COST IN PRETAX DOLLARS = $800.**  **$400. IN PRETAX DOLLARS.**

clothing manufacturers. Included as an integral part of this clothing package are the services of a "clothing consultant," trained in projecting a businesslike image through clothing. In the eyes of the Internal Revenue Service, such a purchase is sometimes considered a necessary business expense to the company, which takes it as a tax write-off. As to the employee's savings, the wardrobe receiver must only pay taxes on the clothing's price, since the I.R.S. considers such garb part of his total compensation kitty.

"Let's say a man goes out and purchases a $400 suit. If he's in a 50 percent tax bracket, he's actually spending $800 of pretax money," explains Senior Vice-President Louis Sinsheimer of Haas Tailored Clothing, the company that "imported" the corporate clothing concept from England to the U.S. "Now if his company buys the suit, it pays $400, but claims the sum as a business expense. The man gets the suit and, instead of spending, in essence, $800, all he pays is $200 to the I.R.S."

Of course, that $200 is in essence $400 worth of pretax income. But the example illustrates that while paying full taxes on the clothing's cost, in real terms, employees only pay the percentage of their tax bracket. Thus, a guy in a 50 percent bracket pays half for his clothes, someone in a 33 percent bracket only a third.

Haas works with retail stores across the nation. Write them at 3425 Sinclair

Lane, Baltimore, MD 21213. 301-732-3800, for the store offering corporate clothing plans nearest you.

## Company Benefits

There are several reasons why a company might initiate such a dress-for-success strategy. One might be to simply use it as a tax write-off; another might be to give an executive a perk; a third, to reinforce a company image they already spend large sums to try to maintain or develop.

When corporate clothing plans first hit the U.S. their tax-break angle was a major feature. However, subsequent rulings by the I.R.S. have "knocked out about 95 percent of those companies trying to use the plans just to evade taxes," according to one corporate clothier. Thus, companies may still deduct such plans as business expenses, but in doing so they walk through a gray area in the I.R.S.'s rulings. Since many companies are audited every year anyway, they feel they have nothing to lose by taking such a tiptoe.

As to the perk picture, many companies previously lavishing such "gifts" as first-class air travel, free financial planning services, vacations, and corporate clothing plans on top executives, have been forced to trim such benefits. But there is a bright spot here. Business wardrobes are considered good perks, because they benefit the company as well as individuals, since the company's image is enhanced by well-dressed employees.

Today, most corporate wardrobe purchases are initiated to combat or enhance a firm's image. This itself is a relatively new concept. But books like John T. Molloy's *Dress for Success* have fast-forwarded the idea that individual and company image are important tools in business dealings. (If a company has legitimate image problems, their tax write-off is much more likely to meet with I.R.S. approval.) Just how does corporate clothing fit into a corporation's image puzzle?

The quintessential example is I.B.M.'s white shirt, worn by all its salesmen. In his book, Molloy details research findings which show that much of I.B.M.'s sales success can, amazingly, be attributed to the "moral" image projected by their salesmen's white shirts. When corporate clothing plans are initiated, part of the package involves finding that "white shirt" that will project a firm's desired message.

A business-image consultant trained in designing business wardrobes is brought in. These image brokers meet with company executives, who detail the profile they wish to be projected by employees. The corporate clothiers then mold that profile, using specific clothing choices. For example, the brochure for Execu-Wear (4801 West Peterson, Suite 412, Chicago, IL 60646. 312-282-7884) gives this description of the company's service for corporations and individuals:

Each year industry spends billions of dollars to package consumer goods, just to entice us to pick one product over another. . . . The same factors come into play in our reactions to each other. . . . In the first few minutes after you walk into a room, your choice of clothes (the way you are packaged), instantly relays certain decisions about you. . . . If we want to be more successful, or we want others who work for us to be more successful, then image presentation is of fundamental importance.

With this in mind we have established a professional service company to offer professional wardrobe counseling to the business community. Our consultations lead to the selection of custom designed wardrobes carefully chosen to help each of our clients toward achieving their personal goal.

Our representatives are experts in color, fabrics, fashion, body proportion, posture, personal life style analysis, measuring techniques, tailoring and alteration techniques. Taking into consideration your current wardrobe, our consultants determine your additional clothing needs and recommend the proper attire, all in keeping with your desired image.

In most cases, clothing consultants don't formulate a strict "uniform" for all employees. "We're not looking to put everyone in navy pinstripe suits," explained one corporate clothier. "For one thing, not everyone can wear the same hue of navy." Rather, wardrobes are formulated fitting employees to the company's image, and to their own images as well. For example, if a firm requires a "traditional" business image, a clothier might use four or five different "traditional" suit lines, or custom clothing, outfitting company lawyers, accountants and salesmen in subtly different looks. Thus, a uniform corporate image is achieved—without uniforms.

## Personal Business

The advantages to the company are obvious. And the advantages to you flow far beyond the big price break. The most obvious being that corporate clothing plans take the guesswork out of dressing for success. Your clothing consultant can explain exactly how your company's top brass sees the firm's image and how you can dress to fit it. Then you'll be playing the image game right and can concentrate on more substantial achievements.

*Corporate clothing programs take the guesswork out of dressing for success.*

Another perk within a perk: convenience. No more wondering if what looks fine at the store will make the grade back at the office. Consultants help select correct fabrics, colors and styles, not only for your body, but for your corporate position. And these people will either visit you at your office, or make a time-saving appointment for an in-store visit.

## Getting Yours

Since polishing company images through corporate clothing programs is new, it's doubtful you're already being serviced by one. How can you make your company realize that a closet full of ultimate office attire for you is a worthy business expense for them? Well, your company may already be compensating you with noncash benefits like financial planning or health-club memberships. If you're in this enviable position it may be possible to convince your superiors to include an office wardrobe in your set of extras, because unlike your financial planning or health-club membership, a sharper you is a sharper company.

Even if you're not in the position of procuring perks, your company may still spring for some of your office apparel. Talk to your boss or the personnel director about such a plan. You may point out the possible tax angle, but don't present the idea as a tax gimmick. Instead, point out the benefits that will surely accrue to the company, as outlined above. If you're in sales you have an even stronger argument, since it's been shown that proper dressing is linked to sales effectiveness. Alternatively, whenever a bonus or raise comes along, you might ask that some of the sum be channeled into a business-wear plan. And, upon moving to a new company, you might bargain a corporate clothing plan into your contract.

## A Breed Apart

Not the corporate type? Even if you don't work for a company, you may still reap the business-wear bargains of company clothing if you're self-incorporated or a member of a chartered professional association. However, a tax research specialist at H & R Block's national headquarters points out that the cases of self-incorporated individuals are judged individually by the I.R.S. If this is your position, check with your accountant.

## Personal Choice

If you become the recipient of this savings strategy, much of the toil of putting together a business wardrobe will be alleviated, much of the fun left in.

*A corporate clothing consultant reconciles the businessman's personal dressing tastes with the image his company wants projected.*

Your consultant will, if you like, make all the choices for you, from the weave of your shirt fabric to the tassels on your loafers. But there certainly can be, and usually is, much more input on your part.

"He tells us how he wants to come across. We present our opinions based on how the company wants him to look. We make strong suggestions as far as color, pattern, styling and weight of cloth," said one corporate clothier, explaining client/consultant interaction.

"We'll tell him his company wants its employees dressing *this* way, and whether the suits he presently owns are on the mark or if they'll have to be replaced," said another. "A man can prepare himself to work with us by taking a hard look at what he already has in his wardrobe. That way, we'll be able to tell what his needs are."

Both said they prefer men to tell them what types of clothes they like and feel comfortable in, and how they want to appear. In this way, your wants can be reconciled with the company's. One way to walk this two-way street: Request that your consultant put together several "right" selections, with you choosing the ones you like best.

# On the Books

In corporate clothing plans, you actually pay more taxes when lowering your bill for business attire. But the I.R.S. also allows a few clothing tax deductions:

• Used garments donated to charitable organizations such as Goodwill Industries or the Salvation Army are tax deductible. When you give, keep a list of the items donated, along with the prices you could expect from selling them—their "fair market value." (You can use three-quarters of their original cost as a guideline, although the I.R.S. sets no such percentages.) Keep such lists with your tax records.

Some charities issue receipts detailing your donation's worth. Charities vary as to the generosity of their appraisals, so it pays to find one who appraises on the high side.

• Uniforms can be taken as a tax deduction if they're not adaptable to normal street wear (mechanic's jump suits, airline flight attendant's uniforms), in which case you can deduct the cost of the uniform, plus its cleaning.

The same rule applies to performers' stage wear. For example, if a singer has a sequined suit made for his act, he can deduct it. Similarly, actors can deduct the cost of costumes and clothes they alter for use as costumes.

*Donating clothes to charity enables you to deduct their "fair market value" from your taxes.*

■ Part III ■

MORE FOR THE MONEY

## • 13 •

# KEEPING IT TOGETHER

## Wardrobe Altering,
## Upkeep and Repair

EVEN the savviest shoppers and dressers can become near mental cripples when it comes to getting the maximum mileage from their clothes. That's too bad. Because if you can get more life from your clothes, you won't have to spend money on new ones. True, this takes some effort. And it doesn't provide the instant gratification of buying the new to replace the somewhat old. What it does provide is cash. As the saying goes, a ten or twenty saved . . .

## Altered States

A major shift in men's fashion during the past decade has left many men in the sartorially wasteful situation of owning wardrobe ingredients that are too outdated to mix with today's current styling. For a time in the seventies, the proportions of men's suits, shirts, ties and pants went the way of the circus fat lady, ballooning to lengths and widths undreamed of before. Without questioning why proportions changed, let's just face the fact that the wide lapels, long, wide collars, wide ties and flared pants of yesteryear today look about as slick as tar.

If you're like most men, you haven't thrown away all of these big-proportioned clothes, because they cost you plenty yet haven't worn out. Well, pat yourself on the back for saving your expensive-but-outmoded seventies fashions, because a good tailor can rescue these golden oldies from the closet graveyard, adding quality items to your wardrobe mix for well below currently fashionable prices.

*Shirt collars with overblown proportions can easily be cut down to currently popular shapes.*

*Jacket lapels are easily recut to contemporary proportions.*

Jacket and coat lapels can be cut down to slimmer and sharper shapes. Generally, you'll want lapels 3½"–3¾" wide, when measured across their widest point. Expect to pay $25–$35 for narrowed jacket lapels, $30–$40 to achieve the same results on a coat.

There are three ways you can deal with shirt collars sporting the proportions of Boeing 767 wings. One is to instruct your tailor to remove the collar altogether, which will result in a casual band-collar style (about $6). Alternatively, he can cut the collar to today's proportions (about $8–$10). Still another option is to discard the obese collar in favor of a new, fashionably proportioned model in a contrasting color. For example, shirts with stripes, plaids or solid colors are easily outfitted with new white collars. And white shirts will appreciate in style value with the addition of a light-blue collar. Such a replacement will cost $6–$10. If your local tailor is unable to accommodate a replacement request, two mail-order operations running "shirt hospitals" will perform such shirt surgery. Both L. Allmeier (119 West 23rd Street, New York, NY 10011. 212-243-7390) and Chandler Collar Re-

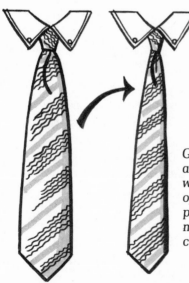

*Straightening flared pants involves sewing a straight line of stitches from where the flare begins to the pant leg's hem, creating a straight tube.*

*Given inflation, even if you add the original cost of a wide silk tie to the present cost of narrowing it to stylish proportions, you're still saving money over the cost of contemporary neck wear.*

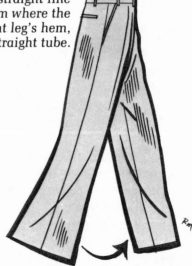

placement (87 Nassau Street, New York, NY 10038. 212-962-7570) handle all manner of shirt ailments and additions.

Even if you add the original cost of a good wide silk tie to the present cost of narrowing it to stylish proportions, you're still saving money over the cost of contemporary neck wear. Today's ties run about 3¼"–3½" wide, down from 5" or wider in the mid-seventies. Stewart Bart, owner of Tiecrafters in New York City, specializes in putting men's fat tie left-behinds on crash diets. In business over thirty years, he charges about $5 for each tie, with a minimum of four ties and a $2 mail-order charge for shipping. (Write: Tiecrafters, 116 East 27th Street, New York, NY 10016. 212-867-7676.) Expect to pay your local tailor $5–$8 for the service.

To take some wind out of your flared pants' bottom-heavy sails, tailors sew a straight line of stitches from where the flare begins to the pant leg's hem, creating a straight tube. Classic trousers measure 19½" at both the knee and hem. Ask your tailor to sew to these dimensions (about $9–$12).

*Note:* A tailor can tack together shorts from pants pained with below-the-knee stains, frays or flares, too. Most pants look best transformed into cuffed walking shorts. Similarly, long-sleeved shirts saddled with frayed cuffs or worn elbows are just begging for short-sleeved reprieve. Such shortening measures may come in handy for secondhand clothing finds. For example, shorts may be made from pleated "pegged" pants from the 1950s. Expect to pay $5–$12 for these changes, depending on the tailor.

# Intensive Care

While updating older clothes into new styles is an option, keeping your clothes in good shape is essential. *Anyone* needing or wanting to beat the odds against saving big bucks on clothing has to win the upkeep game. The first parameter for the upkeep conscious: Don't wait for problems to develop. Keeping clothes in top shape requires a certain amount of daily diligence. Here are some actions to take every day.

▪ Newspaper thumbing and light-colored clothing don't mix—or do, but in a smudgy way. Since you're not going to skip the paper just because you've donned a cream-colored jacket, you might try buying a carton of moist towelettes to use after scanning the headlines.

▪ At the office, sitting at a desk in a position in which you constantly rub against its edge can cause worn spots on clothing. Similarly, you'll wear away pants' seats faster by sitting in a chair with rough upholstery covering. Office workers should also keep liquid or spray-on spot remover in their desks in case of lunchtime spills.

▪ Clothes are like you in that to look their best they need grooming, relaxation and rest. Groom your jackets, coats, pants and heavier shirts by brushing loose dirt and lint off them and from their inside pockets with a clothes brush. Provide your suits with regular relaxation by hanging them in the bathroom when you take a hot shower. The warm, humid air will help relax wrinkles, which may save you a trip to the cleaners. Giving your clothes a day's rest between wearings will also allow wrinkles to hang out and will let your jackets regain their natural shape, often distorted by a day's wearing.

▪ If your clothes crypt isn't well ventilated, and few are, a permanent musty odor can build up, transferring to your clothes. Solution: Tack up a solid air-freshener inside and keep closet doors open when you go to bed, letting air circulate as you sleep.

▪ Clean anything about to be stored. Stains and body perspiration are often invisible, but may set, later making an appearance when clothes are laundered.

## Convenient Arrangements

Nearly all men's closets are capable of "the suitcase effect," whereby any garment stored in them is transformed into a mass of wrinkles a raisin could envy. Increasing creases is one way cramming and stuffing clothes decreases the benefits of your smart shopping, because your clothes don't look their best. Plus you don't know what's what or what's where, what needs replacing or what new purchases would give your present wardrobe mix its biggest boost. If your closet contains jumbled garments compressed into wrinkled blocks, it's time to put your wardrobe's house in order.

A good first step toward quelling closet turmoil is to take *everything* out of your closet and prune your wardrobe of items no longer appropriate. Those that don't fit anymore, or never did, and anything you know will never again fit your sartorial scheme. (Incidentally, taking such an overview helps in purchasing clothing complementary to your present collection and illuminates possibilities for updated wardrobe combinations and approaches.) What to do with these out-moded wearables?

Several entrepreneurial endeavors will turn your old clothes to cash. They include selling closet-crowders at a flea market, holding an apartment or garage sale, or letting a resale shop sell them in return for a slice of the profit pie.

*FLEA RITES.* Selling through the flea markets takes some preparation. One obligatory step is acquiring a sales tax number. It's issued free by your local Taxpayer's Assistance Bureau. To find the best flea for your goods, look in local and weekly newspapers under "Miscellaneous Sales." You can also check community bulletin boards and call the local Chamber of Commerce.

You'll pay a rental fee for a temporary selling space. You'll be charged $15–$35. An average price is $25 for a day. If you want to rent space for a weekend, you'll get a price break, say $40 for the two days. Most flea market managers will lend or rent you a table and/or rack. You bring your own chair.

You obviously don't want to run up big dry cleaning or laundry bills. But running a few wash loads will freshen clothes stale from sitting on your wardrobe's sidelines. The clothes you expect to fetch the biggest bounty will bring in the booty better if ironed into top shape. If you'll be using a clothes rack, put your renewed wares on hangers and transport them in garment bags. Tag all your items with prices. Many shoppers will go on to the next table/rack if they don't see asking price indicators. Also, mark sizes on these tariff tags.

When pricing specific garments, don't try to get top dollar for every one, as more black ink is achieved by a sellout than a few big sales. And don't increase prices on garments holding pocketfuls of sentimental value ("I remember wearing this jacket that night on Loon Lake . . ."). Sentiment has no dollar equivalent at fleas. Here are some sample prices. Adjust them according to your garments' condition and stylishness: For a fair pair of pants, $9–$12; suits, $12–30; sport coats, $12–$20; outerwear jackets and overcoats, $10–$30; shirts, $2.50–$5; ties, under $3; belts, $1–4; sweaters, $4–$6.

Here are some more tips for making your initial selling days smooth and profitable:

> If marketing household has-beens along with clutter-creating clothes, clean 'em up, too. Shiny samples fetch prettier pennies than dusty dregs.
>
> Similarly, bring a tablecloth to create a more attractive display. A little class counts for a lot at fleas.
>
> Equipping your setup with a measuring tape and, if you have one, some sort of portable mirror, will ease your customer's shopping.
>
> Keep pen and paper at hand for totaling multiple-item purchases.
>
> Prepare to make change by stopping by the bank and getting a roll of quarters, a roll of nickels, twenty-five $1 bills, five fivers and two tenners. And keep money in your pockets rather than in a jar or some other easily swiped container.

*HOUSE HAULS.* With apartment or garage sales, the flea market hits home. As far as preparation, pricing, etc., holding a sale from your home is just like dealing at a flea market. The big difference is you'll have to generate your own crowds.

You'll populate your property with more people if you place an ad announcing your sell-off in a local newspaper. As a rule, the best paper to advertise in is the one with the most garage-sale listings. For the biggest crowd, place your ad in Friday's paper for a Saturday sale. Other promotion notions: Tell your friends about the sale; post notices stating the date, time and some of the garments/items you'll be hawking on local community bulletin boards; last, on the day of your sale, post some signs around the neighborhood giving your address and sale hours. Get signs out and displays set up at least an hour before festivities kick off.

*PIECE OF THE ACTION.* Resale shops, also known as consignment shops or

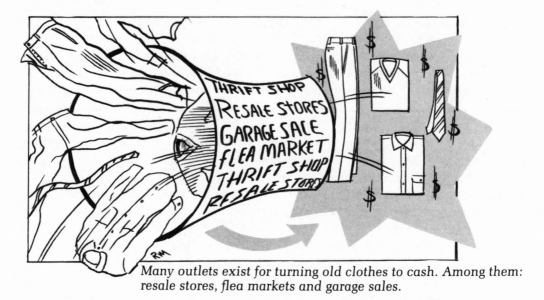

*Many outlets exist for turning old clothes to cash. Among them: resale stores, flea markets and garage sales.*

clothing exchanges, are the convenient clothes-to-cash transformers. You give 'em the goods, they display them in their shop. When your clothes are sold, you get half the sale price. Only half? That's right. But maybe the thought of selling your closet clutter to the public is as appealing as taking part-time work as a nude telegram deliverer. Maybe the convenience of having the reseller handle everything from displaying your clothes to bagging them after they're sold is worth it to you. If so, locate such go-between garment brokers in the Yellow Pages under Clothing—Bought and Sold, Resale Shops, Consignment Shops, or Men's Apparel—Bought and Sold.

If you're lucky, once your wardrobe's dinosaurs are gone your closet will be roomy enough for your most highly evolved attire. But instead of instating your newly groomed wardrobe into familiar surroundings, try these basic storage-space improvements.

• Many problems stem from chaotic clothes hanging or stacking, so you should have an organizational plan and stick to it. For example, categorize clothes when hanging them, with like items such as silk shirts or jeans placed next to each other. Out-of-season and seldom-worn clothes go on the back of a shelf, most frequently worn up front. Fold sweaters and arrange on a shelf according to color or type.

• If your present setup incorporates sliding doors, half your clothes are always hiding. Make them face up to you by installing louvered doors, preferably with slatted fronts for better air circulation.

• Interior designers always design lighting into closets, and you should, too. Fluorescent tube lights work best. However, the battery-operated wall-mounted incandescent models available in hardware stores are another option. General

Electric (Cleveland, OH 44112) makes several different models. Cable Electric Products, Inc. (P.O. Box 6767, Providence, RI 02940) makes Snapit, a plastic light-bulb socket with a switch placed in a closet's frame so the lightbulb goes on when the door is opened and turns off when it shuts.

• Apartment and home builders don't lose sleep thinking about how to make the closets we live with more functional. Very often, closet rods are mounted too far forward, resulting in a gap between a closet's back wall and hung clothes. Remedy: Move such a rod back a few inches so hung clothes come within an inch or two of the back wall. Result: Space is created on the front sidewalls of your closet, where you can install small shelves, storage baskets and hooks—perfect for undergarments, accessories and belts. (More on this closet equipment in a moment.)

• Items stored on the back of a deep shelf may as well be in a safe-deposit box. Turn deep shelves into veritable vaults of serviceability by storing clothes now stacked on shelves on easily pulled out sliding trays. Have a lumber merchant cut these from ⅛″ or ¼″ plywood to fit your shelves.

• Apply storage strategy to the back side of swing doors. A typical arrangement might be a shoe bag mounted on the top half of a closet's door, with several "grid baskets" underneath it. These baskets, in various shapes and sizes, are made from brightly painted or vinyl-coated wire mesh, the wires crossing at right angles as do the lines in grid paper. Easily installed, they form handy see-through drop storage for items usually crowding shelf and floor space. Wire-mesh baskets are manufactured by several companies, including Kartell, 11 East 26th Street, New York, NY 10010; Elfa, 1755 A Wilwatt Drive, P.O. Box 861, Norcross, GA 30091; and Closet

*Apply wire grid systems and hooks
to the back side of swing doors
for convenient storage space.*

*Installing a top-to-bottom vertical partition multiples storage options by maximizing a closet's hanging space.*

Maid, 720 S.W. 17th Street, Ocala, FL 32670 (write for dealers nearest you). Another company, Heller Designs, Inc. (41 Madison Avenue, New York, NY 10010) manufactures a grid system with bolt-on wire grids acting as pegboards when mounted on closet doors. Into these rectangular matrices are plugged specially designed baskets, hooks, shelves and clamps.

• Hooks also help your closet hang tough. Interdesign (Box 39606, Solon, OH 44139. 216-248-0178) makes stick-on and magnetized models that turn unused door and wall space into convenient garment gallows.

• The common rod-with-a-shelf-or-two-above-it closet uses space as efficiently as square pegs in round holes. Installing a vertical partition ends such waste and multiplies your storage options. Here's how:

Take the closet's rods and shelves out. Measure the closet from top to bottom and front to back, recording the dimensions needed for a top-to-bottom rectangular partition. Have the lumberyard cut this to size out of ¼″ plywood. Install the partition, splitting the gutted space into two sections, one twice as wide as the other. (Your hardware man should be able to advise you on the fastenings needed.)

On the partition's narrower side install a rod at a height allowing your longest coats to hang without dragging. On the wider side install two rods at heights allowing you to hang shirts and jackets on top and suits and slacks below. Arrange your garments by color or usage so you can easily coordinate tops with bottoms.

• An imaginative outpouring of "closet furnishings" has become available for beefing up closet capacity. Using such products, a storage system uniquely suited to your closet can be assembled, Erector-set-like, in a Sunday afternoon. Here are some of the better furnishings available:

*REPLACEMENT PARTS.* Ventilated, vinyl-coated steel rod shelving is designed with clothes-hanging rods on the shelving's front. No space is wasted between closet rods and the shelves above them, and ventilated storage keeps stored items fresher, reduces odors, and enables you to view from underneath what's stored where on a shelf. Closet Maid (address above) is the largest manufacturer of such wire shelving.

*ALL MESHED UP.* Along with the wire-mesh grid systems described earlier, under-shelf baskets, shallow with open fronts, which slide into position under a shelf via two U-shaped hooks, create wire-mesh cubbyholes. Heller Designs (address above) makes several sizes.

*STACK HAPPY.* A boon to walk-in closet owners, lightweight stackable plastic drawers provide unheard of advantages in flexibility over conventional bureaus. Their biggest beauty: simple, solid vertical stackability. Most models are easily equipped with castors, making for fast shifts in storage deployment. Kartell (address above) makes several excellent models.

Stacking up a different case are stack baskets. These do away with drawer design, functioning instead as tiered storage platforms. Kartell makes plastic models with shallow, soap-bowl shapes. Stack to desired height to create a repository for socks, underwear, etc. Heller Designs makes a similar product of wire mesh. It's designed with front and back ends open, so stored items can be stacked higher.

*FAST TRACKS.* Track storage systems use wire-mesh baskets sliding on runners built within metal frames. Frames are stackable, so you can choose a combination of them to fit your closet's dimensions. For example, if you wanted to set up

*Track systems consist of wire-mesh baskets sliding on runners built onto metal frames. The simplicity of the system eliminates bulky drawer mechanisms, providing up to 40 percent more storage space than conventional designs. Here, Elfa's system.*

such a system in a 60″ tall closet, you could stack three 20″ tall frames atop each other.

Track systems are most often deployed in walk-in closets as floor-to-ceiling or wall-to-wall stackings. For smaller spaces, baskets can be positioned under hung clothes. Adding castors to such a set of sliding cages creates a rolling see-through storage cart. The two largest manufacturers of track storage systems are Elfa, a Swedish company which pioneered their use in the U.S., and Closet Maid (Addresses above. Write for location of dealer nearest you).

*RACK 'EM UP AND HANG 'EM HIGH.* The most common problem men face in their closets is attempting to stop shoes and ties from running amuck. At times these items seem to defy biology and breed behind closed doors. To keep shoes and ties in good order and condition, use one of the many simple inventions (the simpler, the better) on the market. Your garment repositories' layout determines those best for you.

*HUNG UP.* How to let your clothes hang out in style? The wire jobs that come from the cleaners will probably always dominate your closet rod, but jackets, suits, coats, loosely knit sport shirts, silk shirts and sweaters will tend to lose their shape on those spindly steel triangles. A better bet are "wishbone" wooden hangers with a broader top surface and a shape approximating your shoulders.

If you're trying to optimize minimal rod footage, pants hangers capable of holding up to six pairs of trousers, each on a separate swing-out rod, are a *must*. Shirt hangers holding up to four tops are also available. Lee Rowan (6333 Etzel Avenue, St. Louis, MO 63133) makes serviceable models of each.

The following books contain more wardrobe storage strategies: *Storage: Cabinets, Closets and Wall Systems,* by Jane R. Cary (Harper & Row, $4.95); *Plan and Build More Storage Space,* by Peter Jones (Butterick Publishing, $5.95); *The Complete Book of Closets and Storage,* by Stanley Schuler (M. Evans, $6.95), and *The Closet Book,* by Elin Schoen (Harmony Books, $10.95).

# Wash-Day Clues

If you send most of your clothes to the cleaners, your wash isn't the only thing being cleaned out. A lot of grubby five- and ten-dollar bills are being flushed from your wallet, too. To save money, wash most of your own clothes instead of sending them out.

How to clean clothes effectively? No man should have to cope with the vagaries of prewash concoctions, fabric softeners and cold-water detergents. Instead, presented here is a guide complete enough to get the job done right, yet simple

enough to keep the local supermarket's modern-day parade of wash-day products at arm's length:

*SORTING.* To sort it all out correctly, separate whites from colors, and lights from darks. If you only have two loads, the colors will just have to go together.

*LOADING.* Shake out any loose dirt in pockets. If any clothes are ripped or torn, have them fixed before washing, preventing greater damage. Zip up zippers and fasten hooks and eyes so they won't snag. When making up a wash load, include a variety of items, which makes for better water circulation. And don't stuff the washer full. Overloading makes for poor cleaning and added fabric abrasion.

*ADDING DETERGENT.* How much? Most problems result from using too little detergent. Get yourself a measuring cup. I know, you've never used one, but maybe you've never done the wash right, either. Follow the amounts listed on the bottle/box. These recommendations are for average loads. If you're washing the softball team's uniforms or your gardening togs, use more.

TEMPERATURE. The basic rule is the hotter the water the cleaner the clothes. Use the hottest water that's safe. If not utilizing the hot setting, a liquid or all-temperature detergent will dissolve more easily. Usually white cottons get the hot treatment, colors and permanent press warm. Cold should be used to minimize shrinkage, especially in knitted fabrics. "Delicate" settings are used for washable wools.

ADDITIVES. The two main additives you should consider using with detergent are bleach and fabric softeners. Liquid chlorine bleach works best (follow directions on bottle). But you can't use it on clothing containing wool, mohair, down or silk or on many synthetics. Such fabrics require milder oxygen bleaches. Fabric softeners do more than soften. They reduce or eliminate static cling, make some fabrics bulkier, reduce wrinkling, facilitate ironing and help prevent lint from sticking to your clothes. Follow label instructions.

DRYING. First, make sure lint filters are clean. Second, don't overload dryers, as this lengthens drying time considerably and causes unnecessary wrinkling and uneven drying. Third, commercial coin-operated dryers run hotter than home varieties, so when using them check clothes periodically before the drying cycle ends, taking items out as they dry. Fourth, don't let clothes "cook" in the dryer after the cycle finishes, as clothes will wrinkle and stiffen unnecessarily from such negligence.

# Handy Work

Some garment care labels read "Hand Wash." To do so, use a capful or two of a Woolite-type product or liquid dishwashing detergent in a sinkful of tepid water. Wet the garment and gently squeeze the soapy water through it.

Drain the sink, and rinse the item several times in fresh water. Squeeze—again, gently, gently—excess water out. Then roll the item in a clean, lintless towel, soaking up more moisture. If the garment is made of tightly knitted or woven fabric, it can be hung to dry. Sweaters and other loose knits should be "blocked" to dry. Here's how to do it:

Before washing lay the garment out flat on a large sheet of paper. (You can make such a paper mat from two clean plain brown shopping bags. Don't use newsprint.) Draw an outline around the garment. Wash. After rolling in a dry towel, block the sweater by arranging it on your mat so it matches the previously drawn outline.

# Iron Men

Ironing is imperative if you wash, as sending clothes down the street for pressing would lessen the cash savings achieved through self-reliance. First, however, try taking clothes from the dryer when just about dry and hang them in the bathroom while you run a short, hot shower, or steam them directly by passing a steam iron or a "clothes steamer" up and down hung clothes, about 4 inches from the fabric.

If you must iron, it's easiest to de-wrinkle wearables when they're slightly damp, or when using a steam setting. Care labels clue you in to correct settings, but you should start at a lower setting and work up the temperature range until wrinkles start disappearing like ripples on calm water.

Silk, rayon, acetate and dark-colored fabrics are pressed inside-out, or on the outside using a pressing cloth, such as clean cotton or linen napkin. Wool fabrics are ironed inside out with steam, or with a damp pressing cloth. To iron pants: Lay your pants lengthwise on the ironing board. Now lift the top pant leg up and away. Starting from the hem, iron up the leg on the board in smooth strokes. Keep the iron slightly away from the edge of the pants if they're not creased. For creased pants, iron lightly over edges. If you're ironing inside out, keep the iron away from edges as you move up the leg, and use a pressing cloth on the creases later. Reverse and iron other leg.

To rejuvenate the pants' waist and seat, drape the waistband area over the ironing board's nose. Starting at the front zipper, iron up from the pant leg toward the waistband, rotating the pants around the board as you finish each section. Hang on a hanger with some roundness to its crossbar to keep knee creases from forming.

The trick to ironing shirts is to break the job into easily accomplished sections. Start with the shirt's front panels, at the shoulders. Place the shirt on your ironing board so the rounded part of the board nuzzles into the shirt's shoulder. Tug the shirt's tail to get a taut surface. Iron from the tail of the shirt, up along the shirt's placket. Then iron as much of the shirt's front panel as is on the board, including the pocket. When you've run out of shirt to iron, maneuver the shirt on the board so the shoulders and armhole of the side you're working on is supported, and iron these.

Now begin rotating the shirt on the board so that its side seams and some of its back panel are under hand. Iron them. Continue rotating. The shirt's full back and shoulders, its unironed side and front panel all will quickly fall to your advances. On to the collar: Iron its points first and work toward the collar's center with the iron's corner (using its point may dig into collar).

Sleeve time. First, lay a single sleeve out flat on the board. Hand smooth any wrinkles out. (The pleats near the cuff can't be smoothed, just pulled taut to set them up.) Start at the shirt's shoulder seam with the tip of your iron, and work backward down the sleeve until you reach the pleats radiating from the cuff. Turn the iron, and press the pleats flat.

Iron shirt cuffs from the inside, starting at their outside edges and pressing in, ironing around buttons. *Note:* If you wear a jacket all day, no one could blame you, or even notice, if you only ironed your shirts' collars, cuffs and fronts.


## Marked Men

Chances are you could buy the better or best part of a new wardrobe with the money stains have cost you. This is needless waste, for stains are conquerable. The timeliest trick: Take 'em on before they've set up permanent residence. This means attacking stains as soon after they appear as possible. Many spills will flush away with plain water if caught quickly. If a stain doesn't bend to a water treatment, try the following stain removers. But test them first by dabbing some of the solution on a hidden section inside the garment. If it causes adverse effects, take the garment to the dry cleaner. Stained dry-clean-only items should get professional attention, too. Ahead: how to turn common stains into vanishing acts:

• For everyday ground-in dirt and grime the before laundering spray-on products (Shout!, etc.) are very good (follow label instructions). And before laundering is a good time to scout for previously unnoticed stains, as washing and drying will set some types.

• For oily stains—butter, car wax, chocolate, coffee or tea, cooking oil, grease, ice cream, ketchup, mustard, salad dressing, etc.—liquid dry-cleaning solvent (K2r, Carbona, etc.) usually works well. Say you get some salad dressing on the front of your shirt. To use solvent, lay the shirt on a clean towel with the stain *against* the towel. Soak a clean portion of a cloth in solvent. Then, working from the inside of the shirt, try to flush the stain out by soaking it and rubbing it gently. When the spot begins coming out, shift the shirt's position and use a clean area of your rubbing cloth (to avoid rubbing the stain back into the shirt). Work in a well-ventilated room and don't smoke. If the stain is new and will dissolve in solvent, you will, as they say, save your shirt. Stain still sticks? Try working a detergent paste (made by adding a few tablespoons of water to a handful of powdered detergent) into it, rinse with cool water, then use solvent again. (Don't use a paste to begin with, because water tends to coagulate these types of greasy stains, making them even tougher to evict.)

• For stains from blood, drinks containing alcohol, fruit juice, nongreasy foods, soft drinks, first sponge the stain using lots of cool water. Some stain left? Mix up a detergent paste, or use liquid detergent, and rub this into the stain. Let stand fifteen to twenty minutes. Rinse. Repeat the process if the stain still won't go. If *that* doesn't work, sponge on a chlorine bleach solution of a few caps of bleach to one quart water (after checking to make sure this won't alter garment color). For silk and wool items, skip the chlorine bleach and substitute an oxygen bleach-powder paste.

- Chewing gum. Everyone's favorite, right? Give it the freeze treatment—rub it down with an ice cube. The gum will harden. Scrape it off with the dull edge of a butter knife. Remove any marks remaining with a dry-cleaning solvent.

- Grass stains. If the garment is washable, a prewash soil remover may work. Or you can use rubbing alcohol as you would a dry-cleaning solvent (always checking on color fastness first). If alcohol affects the color, soak the stained wearable for thirty minutes in a sinkful of warm water with a quarter cup of white vinegar in it. Rub the stain gently. Rinse.

- Ball-point pen ink is the stain that has nixed more work shirts from active duty than any other modern-day spot generator. Get it out with dry-cleaning solvent. If that doesn't work, try using rubbing alcohol in the same manner (try nail-polish remover if rubbing alcohol fails). If the ink remains, get tough. Make a rubbing alcohol and detergent paste, rub it on, let stand for five minutes, then launder the article.

- Paint. Removal depends on the type. Catch water-based types before they dry, washing them out with warm water (wet with a sponge if garment is non-washable). Oil-based paints can be removed from clothing using the paint thinner recommended on the paint can (again, as with all these stain removers, test on a hidden spot before using). If paint thinner is verboten, try dry-cleaning solvent. *Note:* Some paint thinners leave stains of their own. Treat *these* as you would for butter, car wax, etc. (method above).

- Ring around the collar. As we all know, something must be done about this, and fast! You could, of course, try the detergent advertised on television that gave this stain star status. Alternatively, prewash stain removers work, too.

## Professionally Speaking

OK, you're a wash-day wonder and a super stain remover. No matter. At times your sparkling image needs shining by a pro, and that means procuring a dry cleaner's help. Find a clothes curator with on-premises cleaning (many send clothes to a factory). This makes the owner directly responsible for what happens to your clothes. Check to see that loose or lost buttons and other minor repairs are handled free of charge or for a small fee.

In addition, find out if pressing includes hand finishing, and whether or not jacket sleeves are stuffed with tissue (this helps them retain their shape and is a finishing touch indicating a quality operation). Also, the type of cleaner you want should be willing to reprocess any item if you don't think it came out as well as it should have. *Note:* The term "French Dry Cleaner" sounds chic, but it has absolutely no relation to the process used—*all* dry cleaning is "French," since it originated in Paris.

Help a dry cleaner do his best work by letting him know where to crease your shirts and pants and by pointing out to him all stains and spots (and hopefully identifying what they are) when dropping garments off.

## Self-determination

Even if you dry clean frequently the costs don't have to run as high as car payments. Two alternatives to professional full-service operations—bulk and coin-operated dry cleaning—cut the cost of a solvent wash. Coin-ops deliver dry cleaning, but that's it. Any necessary spot removal or pressing, which many garments require, must be dealt with on the home front. Still, these machines are money savers for the initiated.

Locate establishments with coin-ops in the Yellow Pages under Cleaners and Launderers. The do-it-yourselfers work best for bulky dry-clean-only items (sweaters, heavy pants, down jackets, vests, etc.). Clean pockets of lint/dirt deposits. Check for stains, removing them with dry-cleaning solvent. After cleaning, remove items immediately after the drying cycle is completed, and place on hangers to curtail wrinkling. Lay sweaters flat on a clean towel. Some open-air hanging time may be required to rid clothes of solvent odor.

Bulk dry cleaning is more popular than coin-op as an alternative to paying a professional's full charge. Clothes are handled by a dry cleaner, who treats them as a regular order, but leaves out the prespotting and pressing/finishing processes. Bulk is a great alternative for dry-clean-only clothes not requiring pressing (items in which wrinkles hang out). Prices range from $6–$10 for 8 pounds of clothes, which come back on hangers and wrapped in plastic.

## Mended Ways

It would be nice if washing your car kept it running like a Porsche in showroom shape. It doesn't. Same with clothes. Cleaning keeps 'em looking great, but if you keep them looking new long enough they'll need a part adjusted here or replaced there. Below are some everyday clothing breakdowns and what to do about them.

• Your dry cleaner or tailor should replace or secure missing or loose buttons for free if you're a regular client.

*New collars and cuffs
can reform
worn out wearables.*

- A tailor can turn many shirt collars that have become frayed at the neck or stained (about $4). Both L. Allmeier and Chandler Collar Replacement (addresses above) turn collars.
- For worn-out elbows on sport coats or sweaters, suede elbow patches may be added by your tailor (about $12–$15).
- Your tailor or dry cleaner can also handle torn belt loops ($1–$2), ripped pant crotches ($3–$6), snagged sweaters (prices vary with damage), and, sometimes, frayed knit collars and cuffs (prices vary).
- For small holes like the ones caused by hot cigarette ashes or moths, consider reweaving. An intricate, time-consuming job, the cost of reweaving starts at about $35 and goes up fast.
- For stains on silk ties, you can try dry-cleaning solvent for a stain you catch right away, but otherwise you'll need professional help. Tiecrafters in New York City (address above) removes stains by hand, cleans the tie in pure solvent, then presses the tie from the inside. Cost: about $2.50, with a minimum of four ties at Tiecrafters. About $3 to $6 at most commercial dry cleaners.

# Foot Soldiers

Since shoes comprise some of the most expensive accessories you own, it's usually worth, pardon the expression, taking the steps to protect your investments. Here are some everyday measures for milking miles from your ground-based foot guards.

- Alternating shoes daily lets shoes air and "rest" between wearings.
- Shoe trees are valuable for keeping good leather shoes and boots in shape. They fill the shoes when your feet are absent, retaining the footwear's natural form.
- Before you put your shoes on, loosen any laces or buckles to prevent strain on uppers or eyelets. If you can't slip into shoes easily, use a shoehorn. A lot of guys storm their way in, breaking down the stiff "counter," which gives shape to the heel section.
- To help prolong the youth of new sneakers and running shoes, treat them with a soil/stain repellent such as Scotchgard Fabric Protector. To keep such shoes sharp, there are special "sneaker cleaners" on the market (available at sporting goods stores).

To wash canvas sneakers, wear them, sans laces, right into the shower, where they can be scrubbed down with soap and a nailbrush. Wash laces by soaping/wringing them in your hands. Or throw sneakers into the HOT water cycle of your washer, putting white sneakers with white and colored sneaks with darks. (Don't wash sneaks by their lonesome. They bounce around, damaging themselves and the washer.) Air dry. Noncanvas sneakers and running shoes can be washed in the sink with a mild detergent, again using a nailbrush (gently) to scrub off grit.

- To polish smooth leather shoes, if the leather seems dry, sponge on a soapy mix of water/saddle soap. Dirt should flush away, leaving softer, more shinable leather. Let shoes dry overnight. Then rub on a good cream shoe polish like Meltonian (expensive, but great stuff) with a clean cloth. Follow directions on the polish tin or jar as to drying time, buffing and brushing.
- To waterproof leather shoes and boots, commercial mink oil/silicone sprays are available. Again, follow the specific product's directions.

Don't nix a pair of well-maintained shoes before assessing how much more wear you can squeeze from their soles and urge from their uppers. Here are some common repairs to add years to your footwear's useful life.

- The first refurbishing a shoe usually requires is at the heels. Ship your shoes to the repair shop when about ¼" of heel has been left on the pavement, and a wear pattern is apparent. Often rubber or metal "taps" will suffice (about $1–$3). The cost of more complicated heel work varies with the shoes and the materials used. Be sure to ask your shoe salvager what your options are—rubber, leather, plastic, etc. Generally, rubber heels outlast leather versions.

• Resoling will be necessary during your shoes' lifespan if they rack up considerable mileage. Again, costs vary with materials and·the shoes' overall health.

• If a pair of foot coverings last long enough, chances are they'll need to be redyed. Home shoe dyes exist, but don't approximate professional work. Have a pro dye your shoes a shade darker, but in the same color family, as the original tint. If your shoes' color needs intensive care there's "re-dressing," which strips surface tanning treatments. Shoes are then redyed and polished. Cost: about $10–$15 to dye shoes, $12–$18 to dye boots; re-dressing is about $15 for shoes, $18–$20 for boots.

In addition to the above common repairs for leather shoes, such ailments as rips and tears, stains, worn linings, broken eyelets, separated soles (when uppers and soles come apart) and ripped side seams can all be fixed.

• Years ago, when your sneaker soles wore out, you dumped the sneakers. Today, sneaker and running shoe resolers peel off old soles, treat shoes with adhesive and attach new soles as a manufacturer would (check local running specialty shops for resoling services). Cost $12–$20, with extra services such as cleaning, new laces and new arch supports included in the higher prices.

• Along the leading edge of shoe-repair technology are rubberlike shoe "cements." An example is Shoe Glue, manufactured by Unique Sports (5687 New Peachtree Road, Atlanta, GA. 404-451-2800). Write for dealer nearest you. The product can be used in both sneaker and leather shoe repair wherever bonding or filling is required.

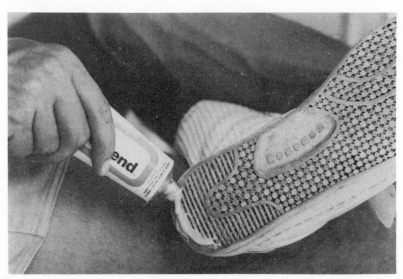

*Shoe "cements" can be used in repairing many common footwear breakdowns, as well as for rebuilding sneaker soles.*

Taking care of your clothes won't make you salivate. It doesn't give you the jollies of happening upon a killer sale. But it will make the garments you're trying to save on *shine on*, which is a master link in the dressing-better-for-less chain.

# IN THE TRIM

## Cutting the Cost
## of Great-Looking Hair

DO YOU GET what you pay for when you get a haircut? You can answer yes and still not be getting your dollar's worth *if* you're paying for a decor transplanted from a singles bar, trendy piped-in music, "free" refreshments, a barber who sees your scalp as one more row to hoe, a "stylist" who has a dress-designer's mentality concerning what you require from a haircut. Lack of experience leads us to believe those performing the rite must be trained and skilled on a level of, say, glass-blowers. Surely stylists must be equal parts surgeon and magician. My own heady hair experience is proof common sense can supplant artistic veneer without causing catastrophe. I used to get my hair styled. I paid about $160 a year for the service. I've since implemented some of the savings strategies outlined in this chapter. Now I don't spend more than $30 a year on hairstyling. You don't have to, either. And unless you wear your hair in a style suited to a Las Vegas headliner, you'll look just as spiffy.

## The Barber's Role

For a while men's fashions tended to warrant a styled solution to hair cutting. The early and mid-seventies saw menswear leap traditional boundaries. Seemingly overnight, overblown proportions were in—lapels ballooned out, ties grew as wide as fists, shirt collars lengthened and flared-bottom pants enveloped shoes. It was an exaggerated, free-flowing look, as befit the times. What was men's

*Today's shorter haircuts have created a back to the barbershop movement.*

hair to do? Always directly correlated to fashion, but usually much slower to change, it took a while for the scalp to loosen up, but soon hair flowed as freely as bell-bottoms in the wind, at least compared to its former length.

Now, as you know, men's fashion has resumed a more refined stance. Proportions have changed, and somehow long hair seems out of style unless you're a professional tennis player. This doesn't hold for everyone, of course. While long hair may no longer be fashionable, it can certainly be stylish. And the idea of men visiting a styling salon isn't inherently bad, in fact, it's healthy, demonstrating men's raised consciousness concerning dressing and grooming. Today, men have a choice.

And a lot of men are choosing barbershop-length cuts, and not because they want to match them to the width of their ties. Today there are more important reasons for wearing a shorter hairstyle. From a business standpoint, this type of hair is the equivalent of a rep tie and button-down shirt. It fits a certain long-established image of efficiency and trustworthiness. In practice, barber cuts are tailored for those on the run. Men can move quickly from shower to office, because short locks can be toweled, combed and dried in minutes. And, keeping them as in tune with today as bell-bottoms were a decade ago, shorter cuts tend to look athletic, perhaps because of their easy after-workout care.

Other inducements offered by the barbershop are convenience and, of course, big savings over stylists' prices. Convenience because a barber will cut your hair in five to ten minutes vs. thirty to forty minutes for a wash, cut and blow dry. Savings because paying $12 to have your hair styled every month means getting clipped for $144 a year. The average barber's price of $3 works out to only $36 for twelve months of service.

Even if your locks have shortened to more classic lines you may be thinking, Surely there's *something* to those stylists. They didn't dupe me all these years, did they? Well, no and yes. To be sure, expert stylists have made cutting men's hair a sort of inconsequential art form. Unfortunately, to reap great benefits you have to find an artist. My hair has seen very few.

But what if you happen upon a frustrated Michelangelo wielding scissors? What do you pay for when you get your hair "styled"?

Unlike a barber, a stylist cuts hair when it's wet, and cuts it a section at a time. A good stylist will blend each section into the section surrounding it. A great stylist will study your features and your hair's texture, and cut the hair so it falls in its natural growth pattern. He or she will create "movement," working with your scalp's irregularities. Because the hair is wet, it can be cut to length more accurately. On average, a stylist will give you a more precise cut, one falling more evenly. But you'd be surprised how little difference this makes, especially with short hair.

You might decide to stick with styling if you are in a profession or peer group where the look is standard, if you prefer the precision-cut look or if you wear your hair longer, covering your ears and extending below your shirt collar in back. You can still save some money by reading on.

If you're opting for styling, go for the best. It pays to search for that frustrated Michelangelo. A run-of-the-mill style cut doesn't provide the qualities it's supposed to. A good salon cut pays some of its way, because each strand of hair is cut the same length, so the style lasts four to six weeks, gaining length without losing shape.

## Search Party

Good barbers were plentiful when your grandfather was your age. Back then barbers were apprenticed. Starting as lather boys, they worked their way up to their own red leather chairs. In their hands, you could pretty much unwind. Today, there are still a lot of good barbers around, but the man trying to find one encounters much the same problem as his stylist-seeking counterpart. It's not so much a danger of falling into the hands of a butcher as finding someone who will take the time to give you a personalized haircut.

All barbers are trained to do this. Barber-school texts stress the importance of tailoring the cut to the customer, much as stylists are trained to do. But think about it. A barber may cut fifteen to twenty-five heads of hair in a day. In his shoes, wouldn't you be tempted to dole out haircuts like so many sheep shearings? Thus, it is necessary to find someone with a bit more dedication.

Your first move, of course, is to find a barbershop. There should be some nearby, or you can ask some well-clipped acquaintances the location of their ton-

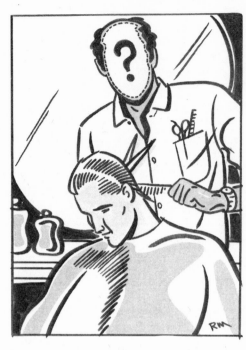

*The search for a barber you can trust won't end until you can relax in your hair caretaker's chair.*

sorial parlors. The Yellow Pages are another option. Invariably, there will be a score of Ed's, Mike's and Frank's barbershops, names which, perhaps mistakenly, seem to have a more trustworthy ring to them than labels like Mr. Hollywood or Style-O-Rama. Forget about the cute decors you've grown accustomed to. The neighborhood shop is likely to be a bit grimy and worse for wear and tear, a result of the large defection to stylists that cut profits for more than a decade. The consolation: Prices are as behind the times as decors.

Most barbershops have managed to stay in business by charging low prices, keeping long workdays and sticking to unposh locations where rents are low. They are usually staffed by longtime barbers, including some forced out of retirement by inflation. The typical shop will have two or more barbers.

How to choose? For your first time back at the barber's, taking the first cutter available is as good a strategy as any. But don't let him just start snipping. Tell him what you want. If you're making some sort of major style transition, illustrate your choice with a magazine photograph or illustration. This is a good way to communicate the general approach you wish taken. Ask the barber's opinion. If he's a pro he will run his hands over your head, feel where the bumps and depressions are, check where the hair is thinning and observe at least glancingly your facial contours.

But what cut will look best on you? Decades of modern barbering have produced certain strategies aimed at creating a symbiotic relationship between your hair and your head. These rules are based on the theory that, as one famous West Coast barber put it, "Every haircut is an illusion, it must be styled to the customer's features." Listing them like parliamentary rules of order may seem too pat, but they're intended as seeds of thought, to sow a field of communication with your barber. Look them over. Do any pertain to you?

• As you probably know, shorter haircuts make hair look fuller.

• In general, a haircut should draw attention away from exaggerated facial features (i.e., carrot-size noses, Dumbo ears, Neanderthal foreheads). A good haircut can't cover up such flaws, but it will substantially alter the face's contours.

• Getting more specific, heavy men usually should have a bit longer cuts. Very short cuts tend to make them look bottom-heavy and pointed on top.

• The same goes for thin men. They seem to disappear with very short hair. The exception: tall thin people, who can look super in shorter hair.

• A too-round face is often favorably offset by longer sideburns.

• Also for circular-shaped countenances: Moving a part lower on one side of the head can transform a round face into one with some appearance of length.

• On a narrow head, a part that starts at the side and angles toward the center back, rather than going straight back, can create a semblance of width.

• Also for narrow noggins: Thicker hair on the sides and hair combed to the front will shorten a long face.

• Square faces also benefit from thicker sides, but take longer sideburns.

• For protruding ears, nothing works better than fuller sides.

Being professionals, barbers use their own jargon. Understanding a bit of it lets you communicate better with your barber. You may have used the following terminology. Now find out what your barber means when he uses it.

*TAPERING.* One skill barbers have over stylists is their tapering ability. This involves cutting the low section of hair on the back or side of your head short (say ⅛"–¼") and gradually increasing the length as they work up. This gives a smooth, sculpted appearance, creating a fuller look.

*RAZOR CUTTING.* In razor cutting, the barber lifts hair with a comb and shaves it off with short strokes from a straight razor. This cutting action gives a super-smooth, blended look. The technique takes more time than a scissor cut and requires much more skill. Consequently, expect to pay 50–100 percent more for the service ($4–$7). Coarse and coarse/curly hair should be razor cut, medium-thick hair can benefit from it, but fine, straight hair responds best to scissor work.

*TRIM.* When you tell a barber, "Just give me a trim," you cede your right to personalized attention (unless you're in the enviable position of having worked out all the necessary styling details beforehand). Be more specific. An average head of hair grows ⅛" every two weeks. If you haven't had a haircut in a month, request a quarter of an inch be taken off. Adjust the figure accordingly, and be specific about how he should handle the sides and back.

*THINNED OUT.* The barber uses special shears to thin hair out. Most men don't need this treatment, unless their hair is thick and unruly. With short haircuts, however, it may be necessary to get rid of extra bulk on top of the head. Ask your barber about the procedure before requesting it.

Let's say you've digested some of the above terms and planned some style strategies before venturing back to the barbershop. But the clipper you get just doesn't seem to care. You admit, sadly, that you'll never transform him into a tonsorial virtuoso. Well, your hair will grow back, so don't give up. While you're in the shop, you might take an inventory of its other customers and their haircuts. Do any look enviable? Look at the other barbers. Is there one who exudes an air of quiet confidence, of composure and dedication? He may be your man, but the search won't end until you can waltz into the barber's chair and relax, knowing the person sculpting your scalp is providing you with personal, professional service.

## School Ways

Clipping the cost of haircuts is as easy as visiting the local barber or beauty school in most cities. There, you're charged a small fee (usually under $2 for a barber's cut and under $5 for a shampoo, cut and blow dry) to avail yourself of a student's services. Can you expect a good haircut? Well, probably. It all depends, of course, on the student you get. Some are extremely conscientious, taking more care than most working barbers or stylists, others are earnest, yet unskilled. There are precautions for guarding against completely amateurish work. One is requesting a student near the end of his or her training, thereby assuring yourself of someone with basic experience. Another is to request that a minimum of hair be snipped, a half inch at the most. Obviously, let students practice their razor cuts on some other soul. And don't request a style cooked up by some fashion forger. Simpler the better. If you find a young maestro with superior scissoring skill, stick with him or her until he or she graduates.

## Model Citizens

A savvier approach to student barbering is offered by some of the country's top hair-cutting salons. There, absolutely free haircuts are offered to "models" for temporary rights to their manes. In some of the larger and more cosmopolitan cities, salons advertise this offer in publications aimed at models and actors, hence the term "model's cut." You don't have to be a model, though.

At these salons, you'll be served (or, rather, you will serve) not a neophyte, but a licensed beautician training in a particular salon's methods. The rationale behind this: Top salons with reputations to uphold must make sure their ever-changing staffs offer a consistent quality of workmanship. Also, top scissor strategists itch to create new hairstyles, but need the raw material on your head to test their theories. The advantage of such programs is that your chances of getting a great haircut for free are pretty good.

There are two disadvantages. One is that you don't have much control over the length or style of a model's cut. After all, you're basically a glamorous guinea pig. The other is that you'll have to adapt to a salon's schedule, which may not coincide with your hair's needs. Finding a salon offering free model's cuts takes some phone and/or leg work. Usually they can only be found in large cities. Reading models' or actors' newspapers is one way to find them. Another is asking women you know if they've heard of such deals. A last resort: calling the most exclusive-looking beauty parlors in the Yellow Pages (under Beauty Salons), inquiring if they know where you might get a model's cut.

# Home Landscaping

As alluded to before, many men imagine that people whom they normally wouldn't trust to count their change correctly at the checkout counter are somehow transformed into beings of enormous artistic skill and motor coordination when equipped with scissors. A misguided notion. Do you know why most barbers take less than ten minutes to cut your hair? Because, aside from special skills like tapering and razor cutting, it just isn't that difficult.

This doesn't refer to someone with a name like Pierre or Justine who holds forth at some carpeted and marbled lair with a name like La Coiffure Extravagante. Usually those people do things with hair that are both extraordinary to look at and hard to care for. But your ordinary haircut, the one Ed or Mike or Frank dispenses, is just solid, if not inspired workmanship. This is hard to believe, but only because you've never tried cutting hair. If you could persuade yourself to try, you'd cut the cost of haircuts to practically nothing. By alternating barbershop visits with home haircuts you'll probably pay less than $30 for a year's worth of clipping, less than $75 if you're visiting a stylist. I wouldn't have believed this, either, but I tried it and have been converted. It works.

You *can* give yourself trims at home. The main thing is not to be intimidated by your hair. Don't be afraid of cutting it because you're not sure what it will look like. You'll only be cutting off a small amount. Major disasters are impossible. (The exception is if you have thinning problems and are using a certain precise style to cover it up.) And think of this: The money angle aside, home barbering nixes the inconvenience of a barbershop or salon visit.

# Head Gear

Except for proper scissors, you probably have the equipment to set up a home hair studio right now. If you have some *sharp* household shears they'll do, though results can't be guaranteed. You'll want to buy some proper cutters once satisfied that this isn't a hoax. A pair of professional barbering scissors will pay for themselves almost immediately. Find them in department or drugstores selling manicure scissors. The best, and most expensive, are made of tempered stainless steel. Buy a pair with blades approximately 5" long; they're easier to handle. Other tools you'll need include:

*COMB.* Partner to your scissors is a good comb. You can use the one you have now, but the best ones for home styling have both coarse and fine teeth and are 6"–8" long. If you're cutting dark hair, a light-colored comb helps you navigate the correct course, as does a dark comb in lighter locks.

*SPRAY BOTTLE.* Your hair will be wet when you cut it. To keep it that way from start to finish, a spray bottle is handy. Use an old glass or plastic spray bottle that has been thoroughly cleaned.

*TWO MIRRORS.* One to face, the other positioned so you can peruse your head's back side. Admittedly, this may take moving a household mirror into position. The best solution once you've become a regular home clipper is an accordion-type shaving mirror attached to the wall behind your regular shaving mirror.

Ahead: how to cut your own hair.

# The Kindest Cuts

A self-haircut savings strategy should start with a good shampoo. Don't cut your hair when it's dry. After shampooing, comb your hair straight back, away from your face, using a wide-toothed comb. The most convenient spot for most men to cut their hair will be the bathroom. To ease cleanup, spread some newspapers underfoot to snare shorn hair.

For maximum freedom of movement, don't wear a shirt. Once facing the mirror, take a few practice snips in the air with the scissors. Get a feeling for their cutting action. You're ready to begin.

*Note:* The following material has been adapted from Bob Bent's *How to Cut Your Own or Anybody Else's Hair* (Simon and Schuster, $6.95), an indispensable guide for serious home hair cutters. The book demonstrates how to give yourself several hairstyles at home. The following "Short Cut" is one.

*Step 1:* Catch a 3"–4" section of hair at the front and center of your scalp with the comb, and, using the comb's gripping power, pull the hair straight up.

Take hold of hair that's about to be cut, firmly between the middle and index fingers of the hand that's not using the comb. Raise this grip to the desired height (say ¼″ away from the ends of your hair), and use the fingers as a scissor guide for cutting the hair. This gives an even cut at the length and angle you wish.

*Step 2:* Put the comb down, pick up your scissors, and using your fingers as a cutting guide, trim hair to an even length.

*Step 3:* Now catch some more hair in the comb, only farther back (but still in the center) on your head, and trim it to the same length as the first section. Keep doing this catch-hold-cut action from the forehead to the back center of your head (it will take from four to six cuts). Use the first section you cut as a length guide, cutting all the hair the same length. (The action is very similar to a lawn mower's cutting all the grass in its path to an even height.)

*Step 4:* Now for the sides. You'll do the same lawn-mower trimming for them, too. First, lay your left hand on the left side of your head, bending your fingers so they conform to its shape. (This will be a slight curve.)

Take the hand away. Now, with the comb, pull a section of hair up and away from the left side of your head, grip it with your fingers using the slight curve as the

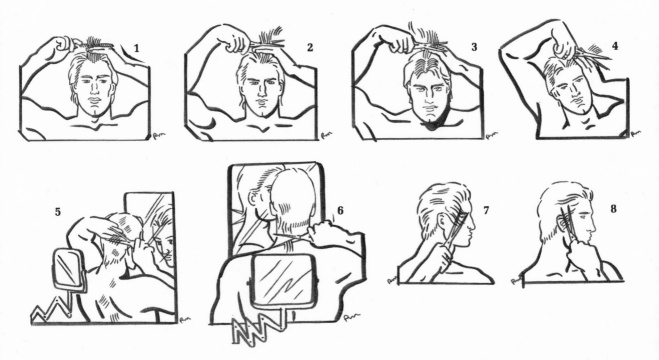

*The steps of a home haircut: 1. Begin at the front and center of your scalp; 2. Trim the hair to an even length, using your fingers as a guide; 3. Cut the hair atop your head to an even length; 4. Use the curve of your hand as a guide for cutting the hair on the sides of your head; 5. Trim the hair on the back of your head, using mirrors; 6. Trim the back evenly; 7. Trim your sideburns; 8. Trim around your ears.*

cutting guide, and clip off the same amount of hair as you did when cutting the center section.

*Note:* The main difficulty you'll have in cutting the hair on the side of your head is matching up the plane formed by your fingers with the cutting plane of the scissors. If you have trouble, try gripping the hair between your fingers very tightly and rotating your hand to the most convenient angle. If you're right-handed, the right side of your head will be easier to cut, and vice versa.

Continue the catch-hold-cut action from the front to the back center of your head. Then do your right side the same way.

*Step 5:* Now for the back. As a general rule, cutting your own hair is more difficult—coordination-wise—the farther back on your head you proceed. And the process isn't made simpler by the fact that you have to use mirrors to see what's happening back there. (*Note:* It may even help to sometimes look away from the mirror and get a feel for the hair between your fingers.)

To do the back, start at the top of the head, on the left side, where you left off before. You'll be able to tell which sections are done by their "blunt" ends. Again, cut hair the same length (remember that image of a lawn mower), starting from the top and working down the back of your head. Do the same on the right side.

*Step 6:* All your hair should be the same, trimmed length. Comb it straight back, and using the mirror in back, trim across the bottom ends evenly. This ain't easy. If you've got a friend handy let her or him do it. If not, use short, small clips instead of trying to hack a straight line.

*Steps 7 and 8:* Trimming your sideburns and the area around your ears is a last, easy step, giving your cut or trim a finished look. Comb the sideburns and the hair below the temple forward on your cheek, using a wet comb. When the hair is spread on your cheek, cut off any ragged edges. Now comb the hair back, and trim the hair in front of and above the ears into finished form.

You won't be able to appreciate the results of your home cut until your hair dries. There's a good chance you'll be pleasantly surprised. You'll probably want to alternate your own work with visits to a barber shop or stylist, but after a while it's possible to become self-sufficient.

## The Neat Goes On

You may feel home barbering just isn't your style. OK, but neatening your own top between barbershop or salon visits is too good a savings strategy to abandon. Filling in for your scissor-shy fingers are mechanical devices putting you in the trim. The most convenient is the Twix Personal Hair Groomer, selling for under $40, manufactured by the Wahl Clipper Corporation (2902 North Locust St.,

Sterling, IL 61081. Write for dealer nearest you). It resembles an electric razor. Equipped with a guide to lift and detangle, and blades to lop off unruly ends, the Twix is simply combed through the hair. Cutting a few hairs at a time, the device allows you to gradually trim your locks without altering your basic hairstyle.

## Treatment Lines

Obviously, cutting the cost of great-looking hair involves avoiding rip-offs and benefiting from bargains when purchasing shampoo, conditioners, and groomers. Here, then, are some ideas for salvaging savings on hair-care products.

*DISCOUNTERS.* While some image-conscious grooming-product makers enforce rigid distribution policies, many have begun selling to discounters. When shopping at such cost cutters remember these points: Many employ sales to lure customers, so stock up on reduced-price items as they appear; compile a list of the lowest prices you've paid for the products you regularly use, referring to it when bargain hunting; watch for close-out goods, stamped with low prices when a manufacturer or store decides to discontinue marketing a line or when a batch of products is approaching its maximum shelf life. Since stores' overhead influences their prices, less-popular shopping districts often harbor better discounts.

*BARBER SUPPLY SHOPS.* These tonsorial trade merchants often supplement their wholesale business with a retail trade, fixing prices somewhere in between. Good buys are likely to be had on combs, brushes, barber's shears and barbershop after-shaves and tonics. Look in the Yellow Pages under Barber Supplies.

*GENERIC BRANDS.* One of the healthiest happenings in hair care has been the introduction of generic-brand shampoos and conditioners. They work like this: A manufacturer unburdened by the costs of advertising, promotion, overhead and large corporate offices knocks off name-brand hair products and offers them at 25 to 30 percent less than their glamorously packaged and promoted counterparts. Almost all the same ingredients are used and the color, texture, fragrance and performance are duplicated to near perfection. A pioneer in the field is Consumer Products (P.O. Box 3457, Grenada Hills, CA 91344. 213-366-7002), offering copies of brands such as Redken and Nexxus. Write for dealer nearest you.

*SHAMPOO SAVVY.* Know the facts. In general, shampoos vary more in price, smell and the way they feel when you rub them into your hair than in how well they clean. And when you shop, how much you pay for shampoo depends on the size and the type you buy and on where you shop. The price per ounce can vary from as little as 5 cents to over 50 cents. The large sizes, say 16 or 32 ounces, are usually cheaper than smaller quantities. And house brands manufactured by drug chains are usually much cheaper than comparable name-brand products.

## ▪ 15 ▪

# GROOMING TIPS

## Shaving Savings/Saving Scents/
## Home Based

THE THINKING behind the shaving products shaving product producers supply can generally be summed up in two words: "planned obsolescence." Saving on shaving involves paring down the wastefulness of this obsolescence by employing the following methods:

*BLADED GLORY.* If you use disposable blades or cartridges, chances are you can curtail the frequency with which you change them, drastically cutting blade budgets without sacrificing shave quality. One research chemist at Gillette has been quoted as saying, "Most people could get a lot more shaves per blade." The shaving studier said only about 10 to 20 percent of all men are what he called "heavy edge damagers," wearing out blades faster than clean socks. But most men are "light edge damagers" who should be able to use the same blade for as long as two months without a significant loss in shave quality.

Thus, if you can change blades less frequently, you'll save money. Holding off on changing your cutting edges for four weeks instead of two saves 50 percent; six weeks, 66 percent.

*DISPOSABLE INCOME.* When Gillette named its new disposable razor Good News!, it really was good news—for consumers. The disposable uses the same twin blades as the company's Trac II shaving cartridges, but costs substantially less. And Gillette's entry into the disposable market isn't the least expensive throwaway. The Bic Shaver, a white, lightweight wonder, can be had for even less of an investment.

*CLOSE CONSCIOUSNESS.* If you don't want to go the obsolescent razor route,

192    STYLEWISE

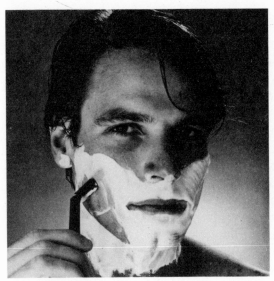

*Disposable razors cut the cost of whisker removal.*

*Solid shaving soaps ensure soft shaving savings.*

there's the electric option. With electrics, an initial investment of $50 to $60 would start saving you money over wet shaving in about two years (based on 1982 disposable razor prices, with a change of blades every ten days). And a quality $60 razor should last five years or more.

Shaving with a blade will always *feel* closer. This is because a thin layer of skin is removed with every wet shave—something no electric does. But unless that close *feel* is the most important aspect of your shave you may decide that saving money by buzzing your beard off isn't such a bad idea.

*THE SOAPS.* "Our shaving soaps cost $3 and last more than six months. That's a lot longer than a $2 can of shaving cream," according to a spokesman for Barbershop, a men's toiletry company producing a line of shaving soaps soaked with scents like lemon lime, herbal, and musk. (Write Franklin Toiletry Company, 76 Ninth Avenue, New York, NY 10011, for mail-order information or the address of the dealer nearest you.)

Getting in a lather with solid shaving soap involves placing it in a mug or bowl, wetting a shaving brush with hot water, then whipping the brush around on the soap to bubble up. Brush sources include: Caswell-Massey, 111 Eighth Avenue, Room 723, New York, NY 10011 (brushes from about $7); and Hoffritz, Mail-Order Retail, 515 West 24th Street, New York, NY 10011 (from about $12); the former also carries soaps ($1.75–$4.50), and both stock brush stands and ceramic mugs.

# Saving Scents

Men with image arsenals containing name-brand colognes pay a hefty fee for their bottled scents. But it's easy to save big bucks on name-brand scents by purchasing your favorite aromas from "cologne reproductionists," who specialize in duplicating popular men's colognes.

These traffickers in the scent trade keep the price of scents sane through a number of means. Most important, they sell directly to the public from their manufacturing plants, eliminating 100 percent middleman markups. Also crucial to lower prices, they let the name-brand boys keep Madison Avenue's savvy packagers in business, because every avant garde bottle shape and glossy magazine ad forces the name brands to tack a few more greenbacks onto their image-enhanced product's price.

Cologne copiers decode the aromas of name-brand formulas using one of two methods. In "gas chromatography," a method of chemical separation, colognes are broken down into their component parts. The analysis shows which major essential oils are present in a cologne, giving the reproductionist a rough recipe to follow in formulating his or her copy.

In the second method used to produce reproductions, a professional perfumer uses his or her knowledgeable nose to sniff out the scents making up your favorite body spice.

Cologne reproductions are not exact copies. The reason they can fool us is that our noses aren't sensitive to the subtleties of scent. However, it should be noted that the imprecise formulas of reproductions, while matching name-brand aromas, may waft a different whiff once worn. Why? Because as you may know, cologne

Reproductions of name-brand colognes
are often priced at less than half
the originals' suggested retail tariffs.

reacts with your skin's chemistry in producing its aromatic effects. In other words, what you smell from the bottle isn't what you smell on your skin. This usually isn't a problem, as the main ingredients, and thus the main reactors, in original and reproduction are the same. But frankly, the wrong chemistry between you and your reproduction may nix the possibility of it replacing your favorite cologne.

Two mail-order sources for reproductions: Pierre Vivion (114 West 30th Street, New York, NY 10001. Write for free brochure) sells 4-ounce reproductions of Pino Silvestre, Paco Rabanne, Aramis and Brut, all for under $5. Jon Paul Perfumers (319 5th Avenue, New York, NY 10016) offers the following reproductions. All prices are approximate.

| BRAND | LIST PRICE (2 ounce) | JON PAUL REPRODUCTION (4 ounce) | JON PAUL REPRODUCTION (8 ounce) |
|---|---|---|---|
| Aramis | $12.50 | $7.75 | $13.00 |
| Braggi | $12.50 | $7.00 | $12.00 |
| Chanel for Men | $11.50 | $7.25 | $13.00 |
| Grey Flannel | $16.00 | $9.50 | $15.00 |
| Halston Z-14 | $14.00 | $7.00 | $12.50 |
| Paco Rabanne | $17.50 | $9.00 | $13.50 |
| Patou Pour Homme | $35.00 | $13.00 | $22.00 |
| Pierre Cardin | $14.00 | $9.00 | $13.00 |
| Royal Copenhagen | $12.00 | $7.50 | $12.00 |

Jon Paul will send sample vials of cologne, containing enough for several days of testing, for 50¢ apiece, with a limit of six samples per customer.

## Home Based

By using natural ingredients to produce homemade grooming supplies, you can save 25 to 75 percent on the cost of skin/hair care. Following, you'll find simple recipes for making everything from hair tonic to facial masks. Most take less than fifteen minutes to mix once you've assembled the ingredients, which are available from the local pharmacy, health-food store or supermarket, or from the mail-order sources listed.

Most of the equipment you need to mix homemade grooming products should be in your kitchen. Essential implements include jars and bottles (save all the shampoo bottles and small jars you presently own) and measuring cups and spoons. Helpful tools include a funnel, wooden spoon, blender and hand mixer.

The major advantage commercial products have over homemade formulas is their extremely long shelf lives (the amount of time a product will last once mixed and packaged). You won't have the luxury of keeping a bottle on the shelf for months. Groomers with a high alcohol content should last more than a month. Fresh vegetable and fruit mixes, however, may last less than two weeks in the refrigerator. To maximize shelf life, refrigerate or store your concoctions in a cool, dark place in opaque plastic or tinted-glass bottles.

*Note:* The sale of ethanol alcohol, an ingredient in many natural grooming formulas, is prohibited in certain states. (Your local pharmacy can inform you of the law governing its sale in your state.)

You have several options if you can't obtain ethanol alcohol. One is to substitute cheap vodka, which, like all vodkas, is simply a mixture of ethanol alcohol and water.

Another is to use isopropyl (rubbing) alcohol, available from any pharmacy or large supermarket. However, rubbing alcohol shouldn't be used in formulas where scent is paramount for it tends to break down scent. So in after-shaves and colognes you'll want to use vodka or perfume diluent. This is a mixture of alcohol, water and scent fixatives. Available from Caswell-Massey (111 Eighth Avenue, Room 723, New York, NY 10011. Catalogue: $1), an 8-ounce bottle costs about $7.25.

Here are the formulas. Ingredients are listed, followed by sources for obtaining them: pharmacy (ph), health-food store (hfs), mail order (mo) and supermarket (sm). For example, "½ tablespoon glycerin (ph, mo)" means you can obtain the ingredient (glycerin) from the local pharmacy or through one of the mail-order sources listed at the end of the chapter.

*Note:* Thanks to the following skin care experts for their generosity in providing the formulations: Shoshana Kliot of New York's Klisar Skin Care Center, Nance Mitchell of the Nance Mitchell Skin Care Center in Los Angeles and Lia Schorr of the Lia Schorr Skin Care Center in New York.

*LOCAL LOTION.* Unlike soap, cleansing lotions can become a mainstay in your skin renovation/preservation program, because they can be mixed for a dry, normal or oily skin type. These terms, seemingly more appropriate to describe racetrack conditions, are the core lexicon that skin care experts use in describing the amount of natural lubricant a man's skin produces. Three cleansing lotions are given below, one for each skin type. Apply them with cotton balls. Soak cotton in the solution, then clean your neck, face and forehead using small upward strokes. Avoid the skin directly around the eyes. Continue until no dirt shows on the cotton balls.

*For Dry Skin*
        1½ cups boiled water
        2 tablespoons isopropyl alcohol (ph, sm)
        2 tablespoons witch hazel (ph, hfs, mo, sm)
        1 teaspoon glycerin (ph, mo)
Mix all ingredients. Shake before using.

## For Normal Skin

> 1 cup witch hazel (ph, hfs, mo, sm)
> 1 teaspoon spirits of camphor (ph, mo)
> 1 teaspoon honey
> 1 cup rosewater (ph, mo)

Place all ingredients in a bottle and shake well to blend. Refrigerate.

## For Oily Skin

> ½ cup apple juice
> ½ cup isopropyl alcohol (ph, sm)
> ¼ cup witch hazel (ph, hfs, mo, sm)

Place all ingredients in a bottle. Shake well. Refrigerate.

ASTRINGENT ACTION. Astringents, which are applied with cotton balls, cause pores to contract, making skin temporarily "glow." Because they tend to dry skin, they can be used during the day to remove patches of excess oil from the face. They shouldn't be used if your skin suffers from drought to begin with.

## Camphor Water Astringent

> ⅛ teaspoon camphor (ph, mo)
> 1 teaspoon ethanol alcohol (ph), or isopropyl alcohol (ph, sm)
> 1 cup water

Dissolve camphor in alcohol. Add water.

## Lemon Astringent Lotion

> 1 teaspoon alum (ph, mo)
> ½ teaspoon boric acid (ph)
> ¼ cup fresh or bottled lemon juice
> ½ cup witch hazel (ph, hfs, mo, sm)
> ½ cup ethanol alcohol (ph), or isopropyl alcohol (ph, sm)

Combine.

## Witch Hazel Astringent

> 2 tablespoons ethanol alcohol (ph), or isopropyl alcohol (ph, sm)
> 1 cup witch hazel (ph, hfs, mo, sm)

Combine.

## Grapefruit Astringent

> 2 tablespoons fresh or canned grapefruit juice
> ¾ teaspoon peppermint extract (sm, hfs, mo)
> ¾ cup ethanol alcohol (ph), or isopropyl alcohol (ph, sm)

Combine. Shake. Especially refreshing when chilled.

MOISTURE LEVELING. On a day to day basis few groomers can help increase your skin's healthy appearance like moisturizers. Dry skin looks gray, flaky. Moist skin fresh, smooth, healthy. Moisturizers work best after a soap or cleansing-lotion application. After rinsing the face thoroughly, use a towel to pat dry, but leave skin damp (you want to trap water in the skin). If your skin is oily in some spots (such as the forehead or nose), skip them.

*Dry Skin Moisturizer*

       1 teaspoon borax (sm)
       ½ cup water
       ¾ cup glycerin (ph, mo)

Dissolve borax in water. Add glycerin.

*Oily Skin Moisturizer*

       2 teaspoons camphor
       ⅓ cup ethanol alcohol (ph), isopropyl alcohol (ph, sm), or vodka
       1 tablespoon glycerin (ph, mo)
       1 cup water

Dissolve camphor in alcohol. Add glycerin and water.

*Lemon Moisturizer*

       ½ teaspoon menthol (ph, mo)
       1 tablespoon boric acid powder (ph)
       ½ teaspoon lemon essential oil (hfs, mo)
       1 cup ethanol alcohol (ph), or isopropyl alcohol (ph, sm), or vodka
       2 tablespoons glycerin (ph, mo)
       ¼ cup witch hazel (ph, hfs, mo, sm)
       ¼ cup rosewater (ph, mo)

Dissolve menthol, boric acid and lemon oil in the alcohol. Add remaining ingredients.

SOOTHE MOVES. Most men use after-shave instead of astringent or moisturizers, as after-shaves combine some of the properties of both. After-shaves are slightly astringent because of their alcohol content, yet contain ingredients that help soothe the cuts and abrasions that result from shaving. (They don't, however, moisturize nearly as well as groomers formulated for that purpose.)

*Basic Conditioning After-shave*

       2 tablespoons of home-brewed tea
       1 tablespoon chamomile extract (hfs, mo)
       ¼ cup ethanol alcohol (ph), or perfume diluent (mo), or vodka
       1 tablespoon glycerin (ph, mo)
       ½ teaspoon essential fragrance oil (hfs, mo) of your choice

This formula is a good after-shave base to which you can add any essential fragrance oil you wish (see colognes for the lowdown on essential oils). Make your tea by steeping four tea bags in 1 cup boiling water, squeezing the bags hard before discarding them. The tea's tannic acid soothes razor burn very effectively. Add the chamomile extract, then the alcohol and glycerin. Finally add fragrance oil.

## Saint Croix After-shave
> 1 teaspoon oil of bay (hfs, mo)
> ½ cup ethanol alcohol (ph), or perfume diluent (mo), or vodka
> 2 tablespoons rum
> 1 tablespoon glycerin (ph, mo)
> ⅓ cup water

Dissolve oil in alcohol. Add other ingredients and shake well. Let stand for several days until solution clears.

## Witch Hazel After-shave
> 2 teaspoons alum (ph, mo)
> 2 tablespoons glycerin (ph, mo)
> ¼ cup ethanol alcohol (ph), or perfume diluent (mo), or vodka
> 1 cup witch hazel (ph, hfs, mo, sm)
> 1 cup water

Put all ingredients in a jar, cover and shake. Let stand until clear.

## West Indies After-shave
> ⅛ teaspoon menthol (ph, mo)
> 5 drops oil of bay (hfs, mo)
> ⅓ cup ethanol alcohol (ph), or perfume diluent (mo), or vodka
> ⅓ cup water
> 1 tablespoon glycerin (ph, mo)

Dissolve menthol and oil in the alcohol. Add remaining ingredients and shake well. Let stand until clear.

SMELL BINDING. Making your own colognes is as simple as dissolving in alcohol, vodka or perfume diluent the essential oils you find most appealing. The simplest recipe: Add ½ ounce essential oil to 8 ounces alcohol, vodka or perfume diluent. Shake.

Essential oils are aromatic oils extracted from the flowers and leaves of plants, and the bark or wood of trees (the same scents used by all cologne manufacturers). They are highly concentrated. For example, 100 pounds of orange peels gives up 10 ounces of essential oil.

Some essential oils used in popular men's colognes are cedarwood (sweet and fruity), bergamot (rich, sweet and fruity), fougere (a fern scent), lavender (bright, heady), lemon (concentrated lemon), lime (concentrated lime), narcissus (sweet, earthy), pine needle (a forest scent), patchouli (a woodsy, earthy, antique-shop scent), sandalwood (spicy, wooded with damp, earthy overtones) and verbena (fresh, lemony, flower/fruity).

Your home colognes won't have the ability to last months on end like commercial products. So if you only incorporate scent into your image four or five times a year they're not for you. An average batch will last over a month if ethanol alcohol or vodka is used. Greater shelf life (months on end) is attained by using perfume diluent. Whether using ethanol alcohol, vodka or perfume diluent, your colognes should be kept in a cool, dark place to keep them fresh.

### Bavarian Cologne
⅛ teaspoon camphor (ph, mo)
1¾ cup ethanol alcohol (ph), or perfume diluent (mo), or vodka
¼ teaspoon sandalwood essential oil (hfs, mo)
⅛ teaspoon lemon essential oil (hfs, mo)
Dissolve camphor in alcohol. Add oils. Shake.

### Plantation Cologne
1 cup ethanol alcohol (ph), or perfume diluent (mo), or vodka
½ teaspoon orange essential oil (hfs, mo)
5 drops cinnamon essential oil (hfs, mo)
Combine. Shake.

### Bay Rum Cologne
⅛ teaspoon oil of bay (hfs, mo)
10 drops orange essential oil (hfs, mo)
1 cup ethanol alcohol (ph), or perfume diluent (mo), or vodka
¼ teaspoon tincture of benzoin (ph, mo)
1 cup water
Dissolve oils in alcohol. Add tincture of benzoin. Stir in water gradually.

### Spanish Cologne
1¾ cup ethanol alcohol (ph), or perfume diluent (mo), or vodka
½ tablespoon orange essential oil (hfs, mo)
1 teaspoon lemon essential oil (hfs, mo)
3 drops rose essential oil (hfs, mo)
Mix. Shake.

CONDITION FED. Natural hair groomers are a high quality savings substitute for commercial brands, conditioning your locks while helping you style them, too.

### Almond Conditioner
2 tablespoons almond essential oil (hfs, mo)
1 teaspoon tincture of benzoin (ph, mo)
¾ cup ethanol alcohol (ph), or isopropyl alcohol (ph, sm), or vodka
Mix together.

### Lemon Hair Tonic
1½ cups ethanol alcohol (ph), or vodka
¾ cups water
1 teaspoon menthol (ph, mo)
½ teaspoon lemon essential oil (hfs, mo)
Mix together.

*Liquid Brilliantine*

>   3 teaspoons sesame oil (hfs, mo)
>   2 teaspoons castor oil (ph, sm)
>   4 teaspoons mink oil (hfs, mo)
>   3 teaspoons liquid lecithin (hfs)
>   ¾ cup light mineral oil (ph)
>   5 drops essential oil of your choice (hfs, mo)

Mix. This hair dressing gives a rich sheen while it conditions. The castor oil in the formula gives hair a firm "set" that holds the hair in place after combing, eliminating the need for hair sprays or tonics. It washes out easily.

SUPPLEMENTAL AID. Following are groomers to round out your image-care itinerary.

*Scrub.* Scrub cleansers mechanically remove a thin layer of dead skin from the face and neck so skin feels smoother, looks more translucent, and has a lighter, more uniform color tone. An additional benefit: Skin is more easily moisturized after a thin surface layer is removed. Scrub twice a week with inexpensive natural cornmeal. Keep it in a plastic jar in the shower. If you use it there the steam will help loosen facial dirt, and there's no cleanup.

*Eye creams.* As you probably know, the skin surrounding the eyes, just under the eyes and from lid to eyebrow, lacks oil secretion glands. While a regular moisturizer can be used on this area throughout the day, a heavier eye cream can be applied at night to fight wrinkle buildup. Plastic surgeons often recommend castor oil. It's cheap, effective and nonallergenic.

*Masks.* Masks are pleasant additions to a skin care program. They can stimulate and smooth the skin and tighten its pores, if only for a while. Once you have the mask on your face, lie down and prop your feet up a foot or so above your head, close your eyes and breathe deeply. Don't leave a mask on more than fifteen or twenty minutes.

*Clay Mask*

>   ½ cup kaolin ("Chinese clay") (ph, mo)
>   ¾ cup water
>   ½ teaspoon tincture of benzoin (ph, mo)

Combine in a bowl.

*Oily Skin Mask*

>   ½ cup fuller's earth (ph, mo)
>   2 tablespoons witch hazel (ph, hfs, mo, sm)
>   1 tablespoon isopropyl alcohol (ph)

Combine in a bowl.

If you have a particularly good health-food/spice/herb store in your city you may not need to mail order any of the ingredients needed for your homemade groomers (look in the Yellow Pages under Health Food or Herbs). If such a store isn't around, the three following mail-order houses specialize in natural/basic grooming products and/or the supplies needed to make them. Ordering all three will give you a good working supply source library.

Aphrodisia, 282 Bleecker Street, New York, NY 10014. Catalogue: $2.50.
Caswell-Massey, 111 Eighth Avenue, Room 723, New York, NY 10011. Catalogue: $1.
Nature's Herb Company, 281 Ellis Street, San Francisco, CA 94102. Free price list.

# CONCLUSION

DUE TO some well-written books on the subject and a ground swell of media coverage, men are becoming increasingly aware and interested in dressing and grooming. Ironically, the high cost of dressing well and good grooming is throwing up expensive roadblocks when men try to exercise their interest and knowledge.

This book is intended to break through these roadblocks, and to open up new avenues to you in implementing your style sense. Its goal is to change the way you go about putting together a wardrobe and obtaining grooming supplies. I've tried to provide all the information you need to dress your best without spending big bucks doing it.

I haven't presented a single formula. Instead, varied strategies have been outlined. You could implement the money-saving dressing/grooming ideas presented here by evaluating your present wardrobing and grooming methods and defining those areas where you could use some new ideas. Or you could just use the savings strategies that most appeal to you.

The choices of how to supplant sartorial squandering with sartorial savings are yours to make. In some ways, the roads to such savings have never been clearer.

# STYLEWISE CLOTHES CREDITS

*Page 20*—Raincoat, Giorgio Armani.

*Page 54*—Suit, Ying Tai, Ltd.; shirt, Sam's Custom Tailor; tie, Michel Cravats.

*Page 59*—Suit, Sam's Custom Tailor; shirt, Ascot Chang; tie, Michel Cravats.

*Page 66*—Sweater, L. L. Bean.

*Page 67*—Shirt, parka, pants and shoes, L. L. Bean.

*Page 73*—Shirt, safari jacket, military surplus pants and hat, Banana Republic.

*Page 75*—Shirt, sweater vest, chino trousers and shoes, L. L. Bean.

*Page 79*—Swim cap, The Finals.

*Page 81*—Silk underwear, International Male.

*Page 93*—Vintage formal apparel, Screaming Mimi's.

*Page 95*—Clockwise from top left: Overcoat, Screaming Mimi's; military surplus French naval officer's uniform, I. Buss; military surplus shirt and pants, I. Buss.

*Page 119*—Right: Tuxedo and accessories, Cerruti 1881. Left: Suit, Hickey-Freeman; shirt, Nino Cerruti shirts; tie, Michel Cravats.

*Page 123*—Left: Polo shirt, Polo by Ralph Lauren. Right: Silk shirts, Pinky and Dianne.

*Page 124*—Shoes, Susan Bennis/Warren Edwards.

*Page 133*—Sweater, Agora Boutique, New York.

*Page 137*—Both photos: Jacket, shirt and pants, Cesarani.

*Page 139*—Left: Rugby jersey and shoes, Soccer Sport Supply; sweat pants, G&S Sporting Goods, Right: Polo shirt, Polo by Ralph Lauren; sweat pants, G&S Sporting Goods.

*Page 142*—Left: T-shirt and boxing trunks, G&S Sporting Goods; shoes, Soccer Sport Supply. Right: Soccer jersey, rugby shorts, soccer socks and shoes, Soccer Sport Supply.

*Page 144*—Left: Soccer shorts, Soccer Sport Supply. Right: Blazer, Cesarani; shirt, Nino Cerruti shirts; tie, Michel Cravats; sweatshirt and sweat pants, G&S Sporting Goods.

*Page 148*—Shirt, pants and belt, Eastern Wear-Guard.

*Page 151*—Left: Waiter's jacket, tuxedo shirt, tie, cummerbund, Scafati, Inc.; pants, Basco. Right: O.R. smock and pants, Bencone Uniforms.

*Page 157*—Suit, Hickey-Freeman; shirt, Nino Cerruti shirts; tie, Barney's New York.

*Page 167*—Hooks, Interdesign; grid and grid baskets, Heller Designs.

*Page 169*—Baskets, Elfa.

*Page 177*—Replacement collars and cuffs, L. Allmeier.

*Page 193*—Left: Razor, Bic. Right: Shaving brush, Caswell-Massey.

# INDEX

## A

Accessories, 122–23
Active wear, 138–45
  fabrics used in, 142–43
  fashion influence of, 138–39
  sources of, 143–45
Advertising of sales, 44–45
After-shaves, recipes for, 198–99
Alterations, 161–63
Antique boutiques, 92–94
Apartment sales, 97
Aphrodisia (store), 202
Army surplus stores, 94
Ascot Chang (store), 61
Astringents, recipes for, 197

## B

"Bait-and-switch," 44
Baker Street Shirtmakers, 72
Banana Republic (store), 72–74
Barber supply shops, 191
Barbers, 183–86
Beauty schools, haircuts from, 186
Bencome Uniforms, 75, 150
Bent, Bob, 188
"Blue-chip" clothes, 121
"Blue-collar" clothes, 146-51
Boutiques, antique, 92–94
Brand-name goods, see Labels
Breakdowns, clothing, 176–78
Brigade Quartermasters, Ltd., 67, 75–76
Britches of Georgetowne, 63, 67, 76
Brooks Brothers, 65, 67, 76
Bulk dry cleaning, 176

## C

Cabela's, 77
Cable Car Clothiers, 67, 77
Cable Electric Products, 167
Camp Beverly Hills (store), 78, 145
Care of wardrobe, 163–64
Caswell-Massey (store), 193, 196, 202
Catalogues, mail-order, 62–64, 67–69, 70, 84
Chandler Collar Replacement, 162–63, 177
Chipp, Inc., 67
Classic clothes, investment value of, 121
Closet Maid (store), 168, 169, 170
Closets, redesigning, 166–70
Coach Leatherware/Coach Consumer Service, 78
Coats
  antique, 93–94
  year-round, 135–36
Coin-operated dry cleaning, 176
Colognes
  name brand, copies of, 194–95
  recipes for, 199–200
Colonel Bubbie's/Strand Surplus Senter, 78
Color charting, seasonal, 130–31
Complaints about mail order, 83–84
Conditioners, hair, 200–201
Consignment, selling on, 165–66
Corporate clothing programs, 152–58
  company benefits of, 154–55
  initiating, 156
  personal benefits of, 155–56
  personal choice in, 156–57
Costumes, tax deduction for, 158
Custom-made clothes
  American, 127–28
  from Hong Kong, 46–62
Customs duties, 57

**D**

Damaged apparel, 111–12
Dasheff, William, 65
Dearborn, Laura, 65
Direct Mail Marketing Association, 83–84
Discounters, 15–25
  brand-name garments from, 22–23
  designer fakes from, 25
  frequency of shopping and, 19
  grooming products from, 191
  growing popularity of, 19
  label-less goods from, 24
  selling environment of, 17–18
  tips for shopping at, 21–22
Donated garments, tax deduction for, 158
*Dress for Success* (Molloy), 154
Dry cleaners, 175–76
  as source for used clothing, 97
Dunham's of Maine, 67

**E**

Eastern Mountain Sports, Inc., 78–79
Eastern Wear-Guard, 79, 148
Elfa, 167, 170
End-of-season sales, 39–41
*Esquire*, 23
Essential oils, 199
Estate sales, 96
ExecuWear, 154–55

**F**

F. R. Tripler (store), 67
Fabrics
  in active wear, 142–43
  in custom-made clothes from Hong Kong, 51–54
  seasonal, 131–33
Factory outlets, 25–34
Fake designer garments, 25
Federal Trade Commission, 24, 83, 109, 112
Finals, The (store), 79, 145
Flea markets, 94, 96
  selling through, 164–65
Franklin Toiletry Co., 193
French Creek Sheep and Wool Co., 79

**G**

G & S Sporting Goods, 80, 144
Gander Mountain, Inc., 80
Garage sales
  selling through, 165
  as source for used clothing, 97
General Electric, 166–67
Generic brands, 191
*Gentlemen's Quarterly*, 23
Going-out-of-business sales, 45
*Good Garb* (Dashoff & Dearborn), 65–66
Grooming products, homemade, 195–202
Guarantee, mail-order, 70, 72

**H**

H. Kauffman & Sons Saddlery Co., Inc., 81
Haas Tailored Clothing, 153–54
Hair, care of, 181–91
Hair supplies
  purchasing, 191
  recipes for, 200–201
Haircuts, 181–90
  by barbers, 181–86
  home, 187–90
  by students, 186–87
Hand washing, 172
Hangers, 170
Heller Designs, Inc., 168, 169
Henry the Tailor (store), 60–61
Hickey-Freeman, 118–19
Hoffritz, 193
Hong Kong, custom-made clothes from, 46–62
  customs duties on, 57
  fittings of, 49–50
  mail-order, 46, 50–51, 55–57
  pants, 53
  shirts, 52–53
  suits, 53
  swatches for, 50–52
*How to Cut Your Own or Anybody Else's Hair* (Bent), 188

**I**

Imperfect apparel, 108–114
Innovative fashion, 122–23
Interdesign (store), 168
Investment dressing, 117–28
  classics in, 121
  custom-made clothes in, 127–28
  innovative, 122–23
  quality and, 118–20, 125–26
  versatility in, 123–24
International Male (store), 80
Ironing clothing, 173–74
"Irregulars," 21, 108–110
  hints on judging, 112–14

**J**

Jon Paul Perfumers, 195
Jos. A. Bank Clothiers, 74

**K**

Kartell, 167
Kreeger & Sons, 81–82

**L**

L. Allemeir (store), 162, 177
L. L. Bean, Inc., 64, 66, 68, 71, 72, 74
Labels, 22–23
  counterfeit, 25
  designer, 23
  removed, 24
Lands' End, 82

Layering, 135
Lee Kung Man Knitting Factory, 62
List price, 44

**M**
Mail-order shopping, 63–84
  catalogues for, 62–64, 67–69, 70
  complaints about, 83
  guarantees in, 70, 72
  measuring for, 55–57
  sales tax on, 64
  shipping charges in, 70–71
Manufacturer's overruns, 16–17
Markdowns, 36–38
Masks, recipes for, 201
Mending, 176–77
Military surplus, 94
Model's cut, 186–87
Moisturizers, recipes for, 198

**N**
Nature's Herb Company, 202

**O**
Outlet shopping malls, 26
Overruns, manufacturer's, 16–17

**P**
Pants
  antique, 92
  from Hong Kong, 53
Paul Stuart (store), 67
*Penthouse*, 23
Physician's uniforms, 150
Pierre Vivion (store), 195
*Playboy*, 23
Post office auctions, 97
Preclearance sales, 39
Private-label goods, 127

**Q**
Quality clothing, 118–20, 125–26

**R**
Razors, 192–93
Repairs, clothing, 176–77
Resale shops, 91
  selling through, 165–66
Retailers
  discount, *see* Discounters
  quality, 126–27
RN number, 24
Royal India Tailors, 61
Rummage sales, 97

**S**
Sales, 35–45
  end-of-season, 39–41
  preclearance, 39

return policies during, 43
shoe, 45
special purchase, 38–39
tips for shopping at, 41–43
Sales tax on mail orders, 64
Salespeople, 98–107
  getting to know, 21, 42
  negative traits of, 100–101
  overtures to and by, 98–100
  ploys of, 100–104
  quality, 104–106
  teamwork with, 106–107
Sam's Tailor, 59–60
Scafati, Inc., 151
Scents, *see* Colognes
Seasonless sportswear, 135
Season-specific clothing, 129–30
Secondhand clothing, *see* Used clothing
Seconds, 21, 109, 112
Shampoo, 191
Shanghai Custom Tailors (store), 61
Shaving supplies, 192–93, 198–99
Sheplers, Inc., 82
Shipping charges, mail-order, 70–71
Shirts
  antique, 92
  custom-made, 127–28
  from Hong Kong, 52–53
  polo, 139–40
Shoes
  active wear, 140
  care of, 178–79
  sales on, 45
"Shopworn" clothing, 112
Skin lotions, recipes for, 196–97
Sneakers, 140
Soaps, shaving, 193
Soccer Sport Supply (store), 83, 143–44
Special purchase sales, 38–39, 41
Sport jackets, antique, 93
Sports apparel, *see* Active wear
Sportswear Clearinghouse (store), 83, 145
Stackable plastic drawers, 169
Stains, removing, 174–75
Storage, strategies for, 166–70
Suits
  antique, 93
  high-quality, 118–19
  from Hong Kong, 53

**T**
T. M. Tom (store), 60
Tax deduction, clothing as, 152–58
Thrift shops, 88–91
Tiecrafters (store), 163
Track storage systems, 169–70
Trench coats, 135–36
Twelve-month wardrobe, 133–34

## U

Uniform companies, clothing from, 146–51
Uniforms, tax deduction for, 158
Unique Sports (store), 179
U. S. Postal Service (USPS), 84
Updating wardrobe, 161–63
Upkeep of wardrobe, 161–80
Used clothing, 85–97
   at antique boutiques, 92–94
   army surplus, 94
   at dry cleaners, 97
   at estate sales, 96
   at flea markets, 94–96
   at garage/apartment sales, 97
   at post office auctions, 97
   at resale shops, 91
   at rummage sales, 97
   at thrift shops, 88–91

## V

Vintage clothing, 92–94

## W

Wahl Clipper Corporation, 190
Waiters' uniforms, 150–51
Wardrobe pruning, 164–66
Washing clothes, 170–72
Work clothes, 146–51
WPL number, 24

## Y

Year-end clearances, 35–45
Year-round wardrobe, 129–37
   colors for, 130–31
   fabrics for, 131–35
   layering in, 135
   trench coat in, 135–36
Ying Tai Limited, 58

HB 7 N